P9-ASL-868

*Dedicated to those countrymen of the Blue and the Gray
who fought, died, suffered and survived
the War Between the States.
We pay our respects.*

———————■———————

George Loomis III

Military History Library

Donated by
George Loomis ⦚⦚⦚

East Grand Forks Campbell Library

MY FOLKS
AND THE CIVIL WAR

*A Treasury Of Civil War Stories
Shared By Capper's And Grit Readers*

PROPERTY OF
E.G.F. CAMPBELL LIBRARY

CAPPER
PRESS

Capper Press
Topeka, Kansas

Editor
Marge Nichols Sullivan

Assistant to the Editor
Patricia Patterson Thompson

Production
Bruce Bealmear

Illustration
Stephen B. Falls

Copyright © 1994
by Capper Press
Printed in the United States of America

ISBN: 0-941678-42-3

FOREWORD

Like the two armies of the Blue and the Gray that waged the War Between The States in a country with its soul split asunder, this book of collected memories reflects two themes.

The first is the staggering tragedy that war inflicts on the generation that must endure it. The second is the shining triumph of the human spirit over that tragedy.

Both will pull at your heartstrings.

This book is a collection of letters from contributors representing two generations. The first is a series of readers' letters published in an April 1961 Civil War Centennial edition of *Capper's Weekly*, now *Capper's*, by columnist Kate Marchbanks. A second series of letters poured from the pens of readers of *Capper's* and *Grit* in 1993.

It is a treasury of authentic memories submitted by real people who have shared their family tales of the unsung heroes who lived and died, laughed and cried, won and lost in the terrible years of 1861 to 1865. The stories come from battlefield and homefront, sharing the experiences of those who waged the War and those who tended the hearth fires.

My Folks And The Civil War is the fifth volume in the *My Folks* series: *My Folks Came In A Covered Wagon, My Folks Claimed The Plains, My Folks And The One-Room Schoolhouse* and *My Folks' Depression Days*. Capper Press now opens the door to another time period with the same immediacy to the era and the emotions it evoked. The opinions expressed are those of the people who lived the Civil War years. We make no claim to complete historical accuracy; minimal updating of spelling, grammar and punctuation has been made to facilitate easier reading while maintaining the spirit and style of the authors.

Step back into another time with us. And join us in saluting those who lived the stories — and those who shared them — with yet another generation of readers.

Marge Nichols Sullivan
Editor

CONTENTS

CHAPTER 1: An Overview Of The War Years

Southern Belle Marries Union Soldier

I have one story about my grandmother who was a Southern belle who went to Virginia City, Montana, with her family upon news of discovery of gold there reaching them in the South. En route on the boat she met a young Union Army officer who was being sent to Virginia City by President Ulysses S. Grant to be postmaster. Although he was Union and she was Rebel they fell in love and married, and lived there through the exciting days of the gold rush — and upon his being injured she was appointed by his friend to the office as "postmaster." She returned with her two small sons to Virginia after his death, and met my grandfather. He had been married to grandmother's cousin, and upon her death, had returned to Virginia seeking solace. They were then married and returned to Nebraska, where they pioneered. She was the only grandmother I ever knew. We children always called her "Cousin Mary Grandma."

Mrs. Leslie Laughlin
Scottsbluff, Nebraska

Civil War Dedication

We think of him now as a feeble old man,
Who nodded and dreamed all day.
As he sat there alone in his old wicker rocker,
Pushed back out of folks' way.

MY FOLKS AND THE CIVIL WAR

His fast-dimming sight, and war-deafened ears,
Wrapped him in memories.
So he'd sit there and dream of bygone years
And hard-won victories.

Sometimes he would tell us an old war tale,
As eager-eyed kids we would gather 'round,
He'd tell how they trampled in wintry gale,
Or slept like dead on the hard frozen ground.

He told us a tale of a brave young lad,
Who shot down a pig as they marched along,
To supply them with meat, which they needed,
Not thinking, perhaps, of committing a bad.

'Twas against the Army rules, you see, wrong,
To fire a shot while the march was on.
So he must be hanged by his thumbs to a tree,
To pay for the wrong that he had done.

The boys were laughing and joking around,
Saying the price was too high for meat.
The General, somehow, couldn't be found,
So they put some stones 'neath the guilty one's feet.

And so, as this tale he told was gay,
Others he told were sad.
Of comrades calling to him, as they lay
For water, when none could be had.

He told of a sun in a hot Southern sky,
Beating down on a field of dead,
Where only a few short years gone by,
Green corn had stood instead.

Again he would tell of great days when,
As their hearts beat glad and free,
They marched along with Sherman's men,
On his victory March to the Sea.

Then marching home in their grime and sweat,
When the long hard task was done,
Thinking of loved ones soon to be met
Forgetting the victories won.

And so, Old Warrior, departed alone,
A few short years gone by,
Down a country lane all overgrown,
With ferns and grasses high.

His horse carried him over the hill,
Where cars could never go,
And it seemed God answered one of his wishes,
For we know he wanted it so.

And today we see o'er a soft green mound,
Old Glory gently wave,
For him who sleeps 'neath that hallowed ground,
Old Warrior, true and brave.
(Dedicated to the memory of John Grove by granddaughter
Emma Elston)

Submitted by Addie Grove
Ingraham, Illinois

The Rebel Colonel

My mother was not quite six years old when the Battle of
Wilson Creek was fought. My grandmother and her sister, with
their children, were visiting that day in the home of their parents,
which was near enough to the battlefield to hear the cannons

roar. My grandfather was fighting with the North and his brother-in-law (and many other relatives) fought on the other side. Both were in that battle. Naturally, the women were very nervous, and Grandmother said, "Just think, they may kill each other."

When it came time to call the children in from play to go home that evening, Mother was missing. At last, one little cousin said, "She went to get Uncle Bailey a long time ago." Just as Great-grandmother was saddling her horse to go after her, a Rebel Colonel, who knew Grandfather, brought her home. He had met her more than two miles from home. She was crying. He stopped and asked her who she was and where she was going. She told him she was going to get her father before the Rebels killed him. He persuaded her to get on his horse with him, telling her that they would go and ask her mother, and if her mother consented he would take her to find her father.

Later, when they spoke of the Rebel Colonel bringing Mother home, she said, "Oh, no he wasn't a Rebel, he was a nice man; Rebels kill people."

> Lillie B. Reid
> Mountain Grove, Missouri

Family Knew John Brown

My great-grandparents lived near Baldwin, Kansas, and were involved in some of the skirmishes of the Civil War. Great-grandmother was alone with her children as her husband was away with the Army. The news was brought that Quantrill's Raiders were to come through there. She loaded her belongings and children on the wagon and drove deep into the thick timber, where they spent the night. What a night full of fear that must have been! The Raiders went north of them, and history tells what they did.

Her means of transportation was a beautiful team of horses, which she badly needed, especially with her husband away. A General and his men came by and wanted to buy them, but she would not sell. That night they returned and stole them.

They also knew the John Brown family. They knew John Brown as a mild-mannered fellow, and not the raging maniac that is pictured today. He brought his son-in-law to their house for treatment of a wound. She pounded slippery elm bark with her "sad-iron" for medicine. We still have this iron which bears the nicks caused by the pounding of the bark. Sometime or other the regular handle was lost off and was replaced by a handle that looks like it might have been taken from a hay hook.

I did not know my great-grandmother, but my grandmother told these things that she remembered as a girl. If only we had recorded the other things she remembered.

Darlene Bruner
Moline, Kansas

The Mystery Of The Lost Jewelry

My grandmother was born in 1856 on a farm near Bells, Tennessee. She lived with us all my life, and I grew up hearing stories about the Civil War. Once a year she would open her trunks and show us Confederate money, buttons off a Confederate uniform, old dresses and dishes and all the pictures and keepsakes of her life. Then she would sprinkle snuff among the treasures to keep out the silverfish and pack the things away for another year.

My grandmother's father joined the Confederate Army immediately and fought all through the Civil War. When the battle came so close to their farm that they could hear the cannons fire, the neighbor women told my great-grandmother to dip snuff to calm her nerves.

My great-grandmother dropped the silverware in the well. At night she went into the garden where she had planted flowers and buried what jewelry the family owned. The War lasted for years. When she tried to dig up the jewelry, she could not find it. Had someone seen her bury it? Had she forgotten just where she put it? I've always been fascinated by that story. Perhaps someday someone will plant a tree and find something of value.

5

The Northern soldiers and the Confederate soldiers were both hungry. When they passed through the area, they would take whatever food they needed and anything of value that they could use to finance the War. The milk cow was staked in a ravine so that when the soldiers looked out over the pasture to see what stock was available, they would not see the cow.

The front door opened against a loom where my great-grandmother was weaving a counterpane. She stored food for her family in the space behind the loom.

Coffee was something that could not be grown in the garden, so they made a substitute out of the skins of baked sweet potatoes. I tried making this drink. It was hot and it was colored like coffee, but I didn't like it. (I didn't like coffee either the first time I drank coffee.)

My grandfather said the most delicious thing he ever tasted was a sunbaked beet. He had found it where a garden had been destroyed by Northern soldiers and the beet had been left in the sun for a couple of days.

After I married I asked my grandmother, who had never been to a talking movie to go with me to see "Gone With The Wind." She refused, saying she remembered the War too well. I have always been thankful she did not go. She would have had a heart attack.

Gypsy Damaris Boston
Shreveport, Louisiana

The Black Dress

My grandfather fought in the Civil War with the Union soldiers. His brother fought on the Southern side. One time they met, passed and never spoke and never saw each other again. I have heard my mother tell of his telling about the soldiers being so hungry a storekeeper gave them a barrel of crackers, telling them they were wormy, but they ate them anyway. When the word came that the Confederate soldiers were coming, my grandmother took his rifle out and buried it. Later it was dug up and found ruined by rust, as she hadn't thought to wrap it. She was a young girl with, I believe, one little girl at the time.

My grandfather came out a Lieutenant, and when he walked in at home Grandmother was sewing on a black dress, and it hurt him worse than anything he had been through.

Mrs. L. G. Hazen
Coolidge, Kansas

Attempted Capture Of Brother

I will soon be 85 years old and my father was a Civil War veteran. He had a large farm near Sedalia, Missouri, and owned many slaves. He organized a troop or company of 100 men, joined General Price and fought at Wilson Creek and Pea Ridge. Then he was sent to Texas to help guard the border during the rest of the War. He brought 50 head of fat cattle into the Army when he joined up. He fought for his beloved Southland, and his brother fought with the Northern Army.

During the War they were called to the bedside of a dying sister, and during this visit my uncle tried to capture my father. He failed to succeed, but my father never forgave him. The little Ozark town from which this item is from has lovely old dwellings which the Northern Army used for one whole winter as a hospital.

My father held no grudge for the Yankees as so many Southern people did, but not so my mother. She could never forget the deprivation and hardships she had suffered.

Not far from here is an old saltpeter mine. In the Civil War days, they came for miles to get saltpeter to make ammunition.

W. W. Ramey
Yellville, Arkansas

War Sentiments Live On

Both my husband and I love the stories of the Civil War. Being native Missourians we have dug up all the facts we can find about our border state during that period. When our oldest son was born we traced our family back to the 1800s on all sides. We have four great-grandfathers who served on the Union side of the War. My husband's great-grandfather's brother was the General who lost the Battle of Atlanta for the South. We have searched the records and read all we can get our hands on of that day and age.

We are living not far from an old Butterfield Overland Mail Station, and soldiers from the North marched along the road in front of our house to the Battle of Wilson Creek. We find few people now days who seem to realize how Missouri was split during that period.

More battles were fought in the state of Missouri than any other. Not major battles, but what the old timers call bushwhacker battles. At one time Missouri even had two Governors, and neither in control.

Always we have thought our sympathy would have gone to the South. To our children we have read stories of the Battle of Atlanta and the General we can boast of, but somewhere along the line they seemed to have missed the point. I guess we made too much of a hero of him.

The other day I found Centennial shirts with the stars and bars flag and the words "Confederate Centennial 1861-1865" on them. The kids were real pleased and proudly went off to school with love of the South and all the facts about Great-uncle General straight except for one of the most important ones.

He lost the War. Just how we failed to make this clear to them I'll never know, and how the teacher explained to our little first grader who was named for Great-uncle I'll never know either, but our little Rebels who went to school that morning so proud of their Confederate shirts came home ready to surrender.

It might of taken a hundred years for the family to be united on one side, but because we failed to make it all clear to9
them, our little Rebels, as they put it, joined the Yankees.

Iris Hood
Flemington, Missouri

"Ye Starved Us Out"

In our town of Broken Bow, Nebraska, there were many old Union soldiers, but so far as I remember, my grandfather was the only Rebel. He wore his white hair quite long, and had a mustache and a pointed white goatee.

I often walked with him down the old Humboldt brick sidewalks from his home on the North side, across the tracks to the town, which was on the South side. Located by the tracks was a huge wooden water tower, painted red. In summer this was an ideal meeting place for the old soldiers to gather and fight the War over by reminiscences. As my grandfather and I would approach the old water tower, the old Union soldiers would call out, "HERE COMES THE OLD REB! WE LICKED YOU, DIDN'T WE?" Grandfather would lift his cane and point it at them, shaking it and let out the Rebel Yell and shout, "YE NEVER LICKED US, YE STARVED US OUT!"

He would introduce me to the other old soldiers, and they would settle down to a long hassle over the various battles, and why they were won or lost. While the arguments would be fierce, it seemed that any real enmity was forgotten.

Leslie Laughlin
Scottsbluff, Nebraska

Home On Furlough

Near the close of the Civil War my aunt and her cousin Frank heard their elders say their Uncle Bob was soon coming home from the War on a furlough.

Neither of the five-year-old children had ever heard the word furlough. In that day no child would dare ask a question at a family gathering. Children were seen but not heard.

However, my aunt and Frank went aside and discussed the furlough problem. How would it look? Frank thought it would be a sort of wheelbarrow. My aunt thought it was a vehicle with an umbrella attachment.

Before Frank's family went home the children made an agreement. The first one who saw Uncle Bob on his furlough should hurry across the field and tell the other about the mysterious furlough.

Uncle Bob went to Frank's home first. How disgusted Frank was as he reported, "Uncle Bob didn't come home on no furlough a-tall; he just come home a-walkin'."

Bessie R. Shinn
Salem, Oregon

Civil War Brings Romance

The Civil War brought romance to my grandpa and grandma. My grandfather's buddy in the Army was killed and Grandpa was ordered to bring his personal possessions home. With them was a package of love letters written by the buddy's sweetheart. Grandpa delivered these back to her and expressed sympathy. They corresponded during the War, and at its close, they were married.

Mildred F. Anderson
Stromsburg, Nebraska

Thought She'd Seen A Ghost

My aunt wrote me a letter many years ago that I never forgot. She related this true story that my great-grandfather Nicholson told her.

"A lady who thought her husband had been killed in the Civil War and had re-married, went to the train depot in Lima, Ohio, to meet the body of her brother who had been killed in the Civil War.

"The first person stepping off the train was her husband." She also wrote, "This lady returned to her first husband."

I often wonder if that happened many times.

Dorothy Nash
Marion, Indiana

Grief Separates Family

My great-grandfather Austin was reported killed in the Civil War. When he arrived back home his mother and two brothers had sold their home and moved away. Neighbors told him his mother couldn't stand to live in the house after he was reported dead. They didn't know where his folks moved to, and he never found them.

Mrs. F. R. Svitak
Hydro, Oklahoma

New Testament Saves Sweetheart's Life

My father was a Civil War veteran who carried a gunshot bullet in his leg to his grave. When 19 years of age he enlisted in the Fourth Iowa Cavalry Division and served the Northern Army for the entire four years.

He was wounded in the leg at the Battle of Guntown, Mississippi, and rode his horse 75 miles, with this wound hurting him severely, to keep from being captured. It took him two days and a night to get back. He tied up the wound with a handkerchief he had received from his sweetheart. I still have the handkerchief.

At another time a bullet hit the New Testament he was carrying in his shirt pocket and glanced off. This sweetheart, who later became his wife, had given him the New Testament when he entered the service.

He came in 1886 to Nebraska. I still live on the home place which he established. He lived to be 82 years old.

Mrs. Walter Binford
Polk, Nebraska

Charity Begins At Home

One of our favorite family stories begins with charity and compassion for a supposed stranger. Grandmother Myers was an invalid during the Civil War and the home, which provided for

11

several homeless "remnants" of the family, was cared for by a widowed daughter with three small children. Besides all the work that was entailed, it was a great hardship to find enough food for all the family members, as they were in a part of the country where much had been lost.

One day the family doctor drove up, leaving a passenger outside in the buggy. He said, "Mother Myers, I have a badly injured soldier out there and unless he can get good home care, he isn't going to make it. Would you take him in?" Her answer was that it would have to be decided by Sarah, as it would make an already hard task much harder. Thinking of the brother who had never been heard of since he was in a fierce battle, she said, "We'll take him in and hope someone is doing the same for Will."

When the doctor carried him in, they found that it was their own son and brother who had been struck by fragments of a cannon ball which buried pieces of his blanket roll in his leg. For months, his sister pulled out the scraps of cloth with a small pair of scissors after suppuration brought them near the surface. Her care and home remedies saved his life and his leg, although he was crippled for the rest of his days.

Mrs. L. F. Sowder
Buffalo, Kansas

A Martyr For His Country

My husband and members of his family often mention this incident which took place during the early part of the Civil War. In July of 1862, a large band of Southern troops came into our county, taking three men as prisoners. One of the three, a doctor, was an uncle of my husband's grandfather.

The story is told in our family that this relative was seized from his bed one dark, rainy night and charged with some offense against the Confederacy. Apparently the charges were serious, for the Southern soldiers killed the doctor during the night. The other two prisoners were released the following morning.

The doctor met his death by hanging, and the elm tree where this took place is still standing. His body was thrown over a fence into a patch of weeds, to be found later and buried. The inscription on his tombstone says, "Died a martyr for his country."

I have heard this story repeated many times; and though the memories have become dim and details have been lost, it has remained a source of pride to our family through four generations.

Marion Aylward
Arbela, Missouri

White House Duty

Family stories about the Civil War are part of my earliest memories. While my great-great-grandfather was a guard at the White House, he kept a diary revealing many interesting stories. Among the more thrilling accounts is when Lincoln called him onto the porch and challenged him to a game of checkers, which Lincoln proceeded to win.

An evening several weeks later might have turned out less happily. A horse and rider swept past the sentry, ignoring his command to halt and give the countersign. After the second command to halt was ignored and the sentry raised his rifle to shoot, the door to the White House office was opened and Secretary of State Stanton said, "Sentry, hold your fire, it is the President's son."

Grandfather survived the War and later he and his young bride went to Georgia to establish the first freedman's school. Later they organized a boarding school for Negro girls.

Paul Bamberger
Hanston, Kansas

Casting A Vote For Lincoln

My grandfather, a veteran of the War of 1812, moved from New York to Illinois. My father was just 14 and his brother 16, so they were too young, and their father too old, for the Civil War.

A neighbor, a Union soldier, came home to vote. He asked my grandfather to go with him to vote for Lincoln. My grandfather told him he didn't think he would vote because the "Knights of the Golden Circle" had sworn they would shoot the first "Blue Coat" that came to vote. The neighbor told my grandfather he was hired to shoot Rebels, and he could shoot them there as well as on the battlefield. So they went to vote and my father accompanied them. He held the team while his father and friend went down a line, about 1/4 mile long, of Rebel soldiers and Knights of the Golden Circle, with their guns cocked, to cast their votes for Lincoln. My father did not think he would ever see his father or friend alive again. They cast their votes and returned to the wagon and they drove away.

I wonder if we would bother to do this; I hope so.

Elsie M. Kirkman
Hays, Kansas

Tripping Troops Make For Wild Scramble

My husband's grandfather was among the soldiers who enlisted in Jefferson County, Wisconsin. Grandfather Chartier used to tell us about battles he was in and other interesting stories of Army life. Among them was the time he saw Lincoln.

The Army recruits camped and drilled on General Lee's land across the river from Washington. General Lee's home was the headquarters for the officials.

On the day President Lincoln and other high officials came to review the troops, the men were marched in front of the reviewing stand. Just as they were going by in good order, someone tripped a man in the ranks — there was a wild scramble; then the men were sent back to reform their ranks.

Everything went well till another man knocked this same man's hat off. He stooped to get it and several more stumbled over him and fell. All got up and righted themselves and the company marched on by.

They were ordered to the front that night. Grandfather Chartier lost a foot in the assault on Petersburgh and later was fitted with a wooden leg.

Mrs. Joe Chartier
La Puente, California

War Still Real After 70 Years

Down along Linville Creek, in Virginia, there lived several families, among them the Lincolns (Jacob and his brother Abraham, who later moved to Kentucky,)J the Herrings and the Chrismans.

Elizabeth Lincoln, the daughter of Jacob Lincoln, who owned slaves, married Joseph Chrisman, and their first son was named John Lincoln Chrisman. Elizabeth died and the faithful Negro servants, Anne and Africanus, helped to raise little John. Eventually his father remarried and moved to Missouri with his family.

John Lincoln Chrisman married, and years later Elizabeth, his second daughter, showed me the books that Elizabeth Lincoln had owned, and also a silver chest. She gave me her father's journal, and patent for the land he bought in Missouri, and a receipt for a slave girl named Millie. During our conversation I asked Cousin Elizabeth, "Wasn't your father's name John Lincoln Chrisman?" She drew herself up and looked stern, "Leave out the Lincoln, please — my father never used it in later life." I was somewhat embarrassed, but persisted with my line of questioning, and asked how she had taught her scholars about Lincoln. She replied, "Lincoln was a Black Republican and a traitor to his own people. I never taught my pupils that he freed the slaves, but I taught them that Lincoln had ambition to educate himself, and that he became a great man because he rose above his early environment."

A picture of General Lee hung on the wall of her parlor and she pointed to it and asked my 12-year-old son, "Who is this?" He noted the beard and quickly replied, "General Ulysses S. Grant." The shocked look on her face made him realize he had made a

15

great error, and he looked again and hurriedly remarked, "I mean General Robert E. Lee." Our dear old cousin commented, "Well now, that is much better."

The War was very real to her 70 years after its close.

Estelle Laughlin
Gering, Nebraska

Children Find Refuge In Chaplain's Hometown

The older folks in our church like to re-tell the Civil War story told them by their grandparents. On a cold winter's morning in 1862, Reverend Albert Hale had just finished his sermon when he was handed a note. He read it, then banged shut his hymnal. "Women," he said, "go home, start the fires in your cookstoves and start cooking for 300 homeless children who arrived in our city this morning. Men, get ready to deliver food and clothing as soon as it is ready."

A Chaplain Springer of the 10th Cavalry, whose hometown was Springfield, Illinois, had rounded up 50 children near the warfare border in Arkansas, put them on the train and sent them to the folks back home for safekeeping. But at every stop, the train took on more children.

That Sunday afternoon the menfolks and their pastor were busy driving up and down the village streets with rigs and wagons, delivering the hot food, warm clothing and loaned bedding. From door to door they went. By night every one of those 300 children was lovingly sheltered in the Chaplain's hometown.

Matilda McLaren
Springfield, Illinois

The Silver Spoon

One of my great-grandfathers fought in both the Mexican and Civil Wars. He was General Robert E. Lee's personal tailor and also cut and made a uniform for General Longstreet.

Another great-grandfather fought in the Civil War. I have a silver spoon given to him by a Southern plantation owner's wife when he stopped at their lovely Colonial home to ask to borrow a spoon to take his medicine. She gave him the spoon, and he carried it thru the War. He died from wounds received in battle shortly after returning home.

There are many branches on the family tree, but somehow that spoon found its way to my mother's keeping, and now that she is gone, I'm the proud possessor of this cherished keepsake.

Mrs. Ronald Longnecker
West Plains, Missouri

A Dream Comes True

This is an experience of a great-great-great-grandfather, just after the close of the Civil War.

When Great-great-great-grandfather returned from the War and life was getting back to normal, he had this dream for three nights straight. He dreamed that in the pasture under a certain bush was buried a copper teakettle full of money.

This Grandfather, I was told, had never been one for nonsense. And, he considered believing in dreams nonsense. But, after dreaming this dream the third night, he decided, out of annoyance and with the thought of stopping the dream, to go to the pasture and dig under the certain bush. He did, and sure enough, he found a teakettle of money. I don't remember being told whether it amounted to much. But, after this experience, Great-great-great-grandfather said he'd never scoff again at believing in dreams.

Mrs. Lloyd Dobler
Camp Verde, Arizona

Neighbors Divided

Among other things my father related to me is the following incident. The community in which he lived with his parents was divided in sympathy — some residents favored the Union cause and others the Confederate.

Two families living close to each other had each a young son of military age. Each of the sons decided to join the Army, one for the North, the other for the South.

Julie Kunkel
Twin Falls, Idaho

Freedom Cheers

After Lee's surrender the boys of 122nd Illinois were marching thru the city of Montgomery preparing to get back home. On both sides of the street the walks were filled with black faces cheering and shouting praise.

One of the women was standing out in front clapping her hands and shouting, "Lord bless the damn Yankees!" over and over again as far as they could hear her. You see, she had all thru the War heard the Yankees spoken of as the "damn Yankees."

Pauline King
Melvern, Kansas

Christmas Greeting

Many of my grandfather's slaves remained with him after the War between the States, and I grew up hearing stories of them.

It was the custom at Christmas for the male slaves to go into the woods and select the largest log they could find to burn in the fireplace as the Yule Log, for as long as it burned they were free to do no heavy work.

Christmas morning the Master and Mistress would have the servants bring the boxes of clothing, extra goodies and other Christmas gifts and follow them to the slave quarters out back. The slaves met them shouting, "Here comes Master and Mistress with Christmas Gifts!" and "Christmas Gifts a-comin'!" Out of this came the greeting that our family always used every Christmas morning. Instead of "Merry Christmas," we would greet everyone with "Christmas Gift." Later my father delighted, when we were grown and in homes of our own, in calling us on the telephone very early Christmas morning and beating us to the greeting. We were wise to him, and we'd shout, "Christmas Gift" first thing when we took down the receiver .

One story we always demanded our grandfather to tell was of the two slave babies who were left in their cradle by their mother who ran away with a Union soldier. My grandfather found them crying in her cabin, and took them to the big house and had them cared for. Their legs were badly bowed and he made splints so that they grew up with straight legs. These little boys were bright and everyone grew attached to them, but about two years later the mother returned with her husband, demanded her children, and my grandfather had to give them up. This was a great heartbreak for the family. However, the boys returned from time to time to visit, and in their adult years they were porters on the C. B. & Q. railroad and would stop off to see my grandfather.

Leslie Laughlin
Scottsbluff, Nebraska

Quantrill Raids Lawrence

The most devastating single incident of the Civil War in Kansas was the raid on Lawrence, August 21, 1863, led by the Confederate guerrilla, William C. Quantrill. The raiders looted and burned more than 200 buildings, killed nearly 150 men and boys and then disappeared into the Missouri hills. Among the Lawrence offices destroyed was that of the *Kansas Weekly Tribune*, but its editor, John Speer, borrowed type from Topeka and published again on August 27. Here he describes the massacre as he saw it.

"We were awakened by the voice of Mrs. Speer, exclaiming, 'What does all that mean?' and jumped from our bed instantly, when a colored man cried through our window, 'The secesh have come!' Looking into town we could see but a small portion of stragglers, the main body being hidden by the building and the densest portion of Massachusetts Street. Soon firing commenced in all directions. We could not distinguish any efforts for defense.

"We seized a double-barreled shotgun, but we found we had neither ramrod or powder. Still, we thought we could wind through the brush to where we supposed our friends were, and get ammunition. The rush of the Rebels to the bank east of town soon dispelled that hope; and we were compelled to return with an empty gun, and make our best efforts for our family. The necessity of securing every person capable of defense compelled the Rebels to pass by all the dwellings on the outskirts of town. Hence, we had time for deliberation.

"There being no possible chance to aid any person outside of our family, we went to work to remove our four little children and such valuables as we could grasp, with the intention of abandoning the house entirely. We had seen so much brutality, had heard the firing, and seen unarmed men falling, that we expected no mercy for even helpless children. My fearless wife, however, said she would stay, but only on the condition that we should leave. We went into the undergrowth nearby. There we watched the proceedings. Previously Allen's warehouse, the Republican office and Willis's Livery Stable were in flames.

"Horses were galloping in every direction, guns were discharged, wounded men and boys were screaming, buildings cracking and demons yelling with every discharge of the deadly missiles. We occupied this position until the ruffians rode to our dwelling. We then passed through a cornfield to the riverbank. Here in amongst the thicket of grapevines and all manner of undergrowth, we found men, women and children, some of the former wounded. Here we first heard that our son was wounded. Men had escaped who had been shot at, with infants in their arms. Numbers of names were given by persons who saw the dead fall, as they fled from the merciless massacre.

"When the cry reached us the demons had left, however, we knew nothing of our own family. Hurrying forward, our little girl met us screaming, 'Pa, Robby is dead!' A poor, sick German woman was at our door with two babes, crying, 'My poor man is murdered!' Mrs. Speer had left to look for the dead. We ran to the scene of the massacre, and found our oldest son shot thru the body. The floor was covered with mutilated dead.

"These details may seem merely personal relations of our own afflictions, but we cannot help uttering them. Would to God that they were exceptions, but they are mere illustrations of the general carnage...the indescribable distress...the agonizing sorrows which afflict the hearts of nearly every family. Women are weeping over the ruins of their once happy homes. We have dwelt principally upon what we have seen and have no heart for hunting up details, especially in regard to property."

Cecile Culp
De Soto, Kansas

Jonathan A. Ross — From Soldier To Quantrill Raider

The year was 1860, and John Ross was soon to be caught up in the most pressing political issues of that era; States Rights; the slavery question; and for him the most interesting issue, economics and the generating of capital.

Early in the War, John Ross saw action at Dug Spring, Wilson's Creek, Dry Wood and Lexington. At the Wilson's Creek battle he was reported to have been the first Confederate soldier to reach and raise the Union General Lyon, after Lyon had been shot from his horse. This was in August, 1861. Confederate forces defeated those of the Union, maintaining a small foothold in Missouri.

John Ross next took part in the battles of Pea Ridge, Shiloh and Farmington. Pea Ridge was a resounding Confederate defeat that ended all Confederate control in Missouri. At the Battle of Shiloh, over 24,000 soldiers were killed or wounded. This was one of the bloodiest battles fought in the War Between the States and a terrible experience for all involved.

The Battle of Farmington was for John Ross, personally, the end of participation in conventional war. Having been sick and unable to do duty, he was confined in a hospital in Mobile, Alabama, until his discharge from the Confederacy. This was in 1863 and his last order as a Confederate States of America soldier came from General Marmaduke and it instructed John Ross to go from Alabama thru Arkansas to Missouri on a mission of recruiting soldiers for the South.

Having finished his obligation as a "regular" in the Confederate forces, John Ross now decided that he could also serve in an "irregular" capacity and thus joined the now infamous group known as Quantrill's Raiders. He was to be an active member of this guerrilla band until the summer of 1865. He is known to have been with the gang on several of their raids and to have been involved in a number of situations when murders were said to have occurred. He was a member of the group that dressed in Union Army uniforms and infiltrated the Northern lines for purposes of sabotage and raising havoc.

John Ross was a survivor of the shoot-out in which Quantrill was mortally wounded. Seeing the situation as impossible, Quantrill yelled that it was "every man for himself," and consequently John Ross, William Hulse, Allen Parmer, Bud Perce and Lee McMurtry shot their way to freedom. It is interesting to note that Parmer was Jesse James's brother-in-law, and like Frank and Jesse James, a personal friend of John Ross.

On July 26, 1865, John Ross and Frank James surrendered to federal authorities at Samuels Depot in Nelson County, Kentucky. They were later granted a pardon.

Althea Fifield Kendall
Pullman, Washington

Sharpshooter Nails Jonathan Ross's Cup

Anne Luella Ledington was born 26 May, 1878, to Elijah and Mary Ann Garrett Ledington at Onaga in Pottawatomie County, Kansas. Mary Ann's father was Reverend Elder William Caldwell Garrett. He was a well-known and respected Baptist minister.

He presided at the marriage of his daughter and Elijah. They were married after Elijah returned from serving in the Union Army during the Civil War.

Elijah's company was among the first to be issued the Sharps rifle, this and the Mississippi rifle were the most accurate guns available to the Union Forces. The men who used the Sharps rifle were called "sharpshooters." Elijah was considered as one of the best and was often sent out to scout or spy for the Army.

A story in family history was often told at family gatherings. Elijah's daughter, Anne, had married John A. Ross and John's father and Elijah were "swapping war stories." Elijah told how in the Missouri campaign, he came upon a group of Confederate soldiers seated around a campfire. He enjoyed a good laugh when he shot a cup out of the hand of one of the Rebels. Jonathan Ross's response was, "I was the one holding that cup." The situation almost became physical!

It is very probable that this did indeed happen since Elijah and Jonathan had opposed each other in several battles in the Missouri-Price campaign.

Althea Fifield Kendall
Pullman, Washington

Borden's Eagle Brand Condensed Milk

My husband's great-uncle, Gail Borden (1777-1863), lived in Galveston, Texas, in his earlier years, until he began experimenting with ways to preserve food items. He had little success, however, until his two young sons inadvertently led him to the idea that established his fame and fortune.

In the middle 1800s, Gail's children were preparing their lunch pails to carry to school. They also carried a small pail of milk to drink. One son had his mother put sugar in the milk he carried, but the other wanted his natural. After school that evening, their father noticed that they each had a bit of milk remaining. Gail tasted the milk and discovered that the unsweetened milk had soured, but the sweetened milk was fresh and unspoiled. With this breakthrough discovery, he began processing what is now known as condensed milk.

A magazine article in the late 1800s had this to say regarding Gail Borden's invention: "The first organization of Gail Borden's valuable invention took the title of Borden's Condensed Milk Company. The Civil War precipitated upon the company very heavy demands for its product, and the Northern Armies were supplied as extensively as manufacturing facilities would permit. It was a happy day when the Southern soldiers were lucky enough to get access to the Union supply train, and thereby obtain what was eagerly sought for by all the soldiers, namely Borden's Eagle Brand Condensed Milk. This popular brand of milk has been the standby of the day and the most valuable food product which the soldier in the field or the sailor at sea can obtain. Lt. Perry testified very highly of its value, and his expedition was well supplied with this indispensable article of food."

Mrs. Morris Borden Tucker
Oklahoma City, Oklahoma

Dungarees And Overalls

My great-grandfather, Fleming Waterfield, was a Civil War veteran. For many years his great-grandchildren were told he was too young to serve in the Civil War. He accompanied the Calvary troops to help with the horses.

As we great-grandchildren grew older, knowing F. W. was born in 1832, when the Civil War started he was nearly 30 years old. Later stories leaked out that F. W. and his brother Jack were thrown in a dungeon, taken prisoner, I presume.

Fleming Waterfield had a first cousin in Howard County by the same name who served in the Confederate Army. While searching for scraps of information, it was impossible for any relative to admit F. W. served in the Confederate Army. They were taught to remain silent on Civil War matters.

They also told how many North or South sympathizers could be identified even today. The Northerners wore blue dungarees; Southerners wore what I always thought were striped carpenter overalls.

> Louise Foster
> Moberly, Missouri

Army Beans

Father had been a Union soldier and like the rest was a radical one. There was a G.A.R. (Grand Army of the Republic) Post and on Memorial Day hundreds of G.A.R. veterans would fall in line, four abreast, and march to the cemetery to the drum and bugle corps music. They each carried a bouquet, and Old Glory and their Post flag waved proudly.

How I loved that marching. And to hear the singing! Such songs as "Tenting Tonight on the Old Campground" and "Just before the Battle, Mother". Then when they got together for a party, they would sing this to the tune of "Sweet By and By."

"Army beans, good old beans
Good for boil, bake or broil, roast or fry
Eat 'em now, anyhow
Scrape the pan, if you can
By and By."

> Mrs. Edith Elder
> Oregon, Missouri

Wife Blinded By Soldier Husband's Infection

Although I do not know the birthdate of my maternal great-great-grandfather, Tyre Mutchler, I know that he fought in the Civil War as one of my cousins shared her own treasure trove of information, which included my great-great-grandfather's Civil War records and pictures of my great-great-grandmother, Lucinda Singleton-Mutchler, who went blind as a direct result of caring for her husband who suffered intestinal fever, severe diarrhea and a gunshot wound before being released on sick leave on January 2, 1864, after having joined the 10th Regiment of the Army in Indiana, having enrolled at Indianapolis on the 18th day of September, 1861.

He died at home on May 2, 1864, still on sick leave from the Army at Clinton County, Indiana. His wife applied for and received not only a Civil War Widows' pension but a blind pension as well.

Because my great-great-grandmother played her part in the Civil War it should be noted that she was a determined little woman — an immaculate housekeeper, even after going blind — and measured 4 feet 10 inches tall and wore such a tiny shoe that it was almost impossible to fit her with shoes.

Sarah Hudson-Pierce
Plain Dealing, Louisiana

Newspaper Article Tells Of Union Vet's White House Visit
Washington, Feb 12 (AP)

"A 93-year-old Pennsylvanian, only survivor of President Abraham Lincoln's last bodyguard, was received at the White House by President (Theodore) Roosevelt Tuesday, as part of the chief executive's observance of the Emancipator's birthday.

The veteran was William Henry Gilbert of Craley, Pa., one of six Union soldiers who guarded Lincoln's bier at Philadelphia where the body lay in state before being taken to Illinois for burial.

Wearing the uniform of the "boys in blue," Gilbert was introduced to President Roosevelt by Representative Haines, Democrat, Pennsylvania. During the interview, Gilbert sat in one of Lincoln's cabinet chairs and viewed the famous Lincoln bed.

Leaving the White House, Gilbert went to the Lincoln Memorial and joined in memorial exercises there. As he climbed slowly the long flight of steps to the statue of his former commander, the Marine Band played DeKoven's 'Recessional'."

The age of William Henry Gilbert and that of my father, James Henry Gilbert, and the fact that Henry is used in the family name over and over, suggests that the Civil War vet could be my grandfather.

Russell H. Gilbert
Hopkins, Minnesota

North-South Couple Disowned By Both Families

My great-great-uncle, Melville Landon, was a young Treasury clerk in Washington, D.C., when the Civil War began. He helped General Cassius Marcellus Clay to organize the "Clay Battalion" to defend the President until federal troops could reach the Capitol. He served in its ranks and later resigned his Treasury position to accept a position on the staff of Gen. A. L. Chitlain commanding the post of Memphis, Tennessee.

As with so many families, we also had ancestors serving in the Confederate Army. My maternal great-grandfather, John Glanton, was a Georgia volunteer. He was badly injured, and died in 1870, never living to see his only child (my grandmother) who was born after his death.

A footnote: My maternal great-grandmother was a widow at the time of the Civil War. She fell in love with a Union soldier and both his and her families disowned them.

Mrs. Ralph Lindsay
Lancaster, California

Fear Of Shooting Family

Grandpa was always afraid he would shoot Uncle John while both were serving in the Civil War. Grandfather served on the Union side, and Uncle John served in the Confederate Army.

Pauline Fecht
Syracuse, Kansas

Friendship Between The Trenches

I'm sure it was not true in all places, but I have heard my grandfather tell about Union and Rebel soldiers being friendly with each other, when there was no battle being fought.

They would come out of their trenches, when the lines were close, lie in the sun and talk to each other, sometimes exchanging chewing tobacco. Then someone would say, "Well, it's about time for the battle to start; everyone hunt his hole." Then the shooting would start.

It was not unusual for civilians to come out and watch the fighting. Occasionally a man would bring his musket, get in a few shots and go back home.

In some cases, under a flag of truce, each side would pick up the dead and wounded, then resume the battle. Sometimes they would even borrow shovels from each other to bury their dead.

The Rebels also dug trenches and rifle pits while they had the shovels. It wasn't unusual during a lull in battle for both sides to pick blackberries, gather wild onions or get anything else they could find to eat between the lines.

Often a stream divided the battlegrounds and during a "quiet," men from each side would bathe in the stream at the same time. All this was forbidden by the officers but there probably has never been another army where individuals made as many decisions for themselves.

There was an often-told story of a Rebel Chaplain baptizing some soldiers in a stream when the Yankees came down on their side and joined in the singing.

To listen to the oldtimers it would seem that soldiers respected each other as individuals but hated each other as armies. It wasn't unheard of for Yankees and Rebels to meet in a "sheltered spot" and play cards and not unusual for a Rebel to return to his lines with a coat, blanket or knife that he had won. When they had nothing else left to gamble with, they were sometimes known to steal a chicken to get in a card with.

At one time when the Rebel and Yankee trenches were real close together, the Yankees were throwing some type of mortar shells into the Rebel trenches, so two men would hold a blanket over the heads of the riflemen down the length of the trench. When the shells fell on the blanket they would "flip" them back toward the Yankee trenches. It was about as serious as any encounter could be.

After several hours when most of the men were wondering if any of them would come out of it alive, one of the blanketmen, Matthew Fulgham, said, "Boys, if this keeps up it's going to get real dangerous." That started the men to laughing and they "went over the top" and routed the Yankees.

An excerpt from *As I Remember It Stories of Civil War Times.*

> B. C. Harpole, Author
> West Point, Mississippi

Honeymoon On A Gunboat

My great-grandfather, Charles Gardner Coffin, captained ships plying the northeastern coastal waters. During the Civil War, he was commissioned by Gideon Wells, Lincoln's Secretary of the Navy, to "Transmit Troops Under the Guns of the Potomac" and to carry armaments and other supplies for the Union Army; often operating under crossfire between the Armies of the Union and the Confederacy.

The following is an excerpt from a rather lengthy letter he wrote in February of 1861, while he and his Annie were on their honeymoon.

> Providence
> Feby. 6th 1861

Dear Aunt Carrie,

We this morning received your letter and were very much pleased to hear from home. Annie says it seems as if we had been gone from home two months and she cannot realize that it was only a week ago since we were married in New York.

It was so blustering and cold about those guns which were fired for us and attracted the attention of all the passengers, who remarked that possibly the secessionists were taking the city.

I had a notion to tell them that they were in honor of the triumph of Union Principles, and if they asked how, I could have bid them look at those TWO people before them who had just been made ONE.

Your Nephew, Charlie

Hudson, New York
March 30th, 1862

My Dear Aunty,

The river (Hudson) is closed to all but a few. Charlie goes down to bring back the boat for re-loading, and I am fortunate to be able to travel with him this time.

Our wardrobes need replenishing, not an easy task with things in such short supply. This war has made more of an impact on our lives than one would have imagined, since the actual turmoil is so far removed.

If the river had been open we should have gone to New York tonight, but now we shall have to wait until Tuesday night. I sadly fear I shall not be able to see anyone socially during our stay and only expect to concentrate on gowns and fittings for two or three days. There is so much to accomplish in that time.

If you happen to arrive in New York Wednesday, do drop in to Mr. Hunt's; you may find us there if the boats are running, and we would truly enjoy your company.

Your affectionate niece,
Annie E. Coffin

Note: In 1862, Annie was about 21 and Charlie must have been nearly 25. "Captain Charlie" and his "boat" were appointed to "Serve the Union Forces at the Pleasure of the Secretary of the Navy."

Sara Hewitt Riola
Lakewood, New Jersey

CHAPTER 2: Signing Up For The Cause

The Measure Of A Man

My father was a Civil War veteran. He was born in the state of Pennsylvania, and when the Civil War broke out in 1861, he was only 17 years old. He wasn't quite tall enough either, but he was eager to get in the Army and do his duty for his country.

With the consent of his father, he could overcome the lack in years, but not the lack of height. The officer that measured the soldiers was a friend of Father's, and because there wasn't sufficient time to measure each boy separate, the officer just stood the men in a line.

Then the officer used a pole five and one-half feet long, which was the required height, then stood the pole on end, and looked over it at the line of men to see that none were too short.

The officer kept Father in one line while he measured other lines, then slipped Father to a line he had already measured. That way he wasn't measured at all.

He was passed to become a bugle boy, but as soldiers were needed so badly, he enlisted as a soldier.

He went all through the Civil War and witnessed Lee's surrender to General Grant at Appomattox, Virginia, April 9, 1865.

The soldiers fired 100 rounds of minute rifles as a salute to Lincoln after he was assassinated.

Laura Dyken
Smith Center, Kansas

Better Late Than Never

Here is an interesting story concerning my grandfather who served in the Civil War.

At 16 his folks wanted him to stay at home, but he was insistent on joining the Union Army. One day his mother sent him for an armload of wood, and instead of bringing the wood, he ran away and enlisted. He served three years, part of which was under General Sherman, and then came home carrying the wood his mother had ordered three years before.

Mrs. T. W. Neil
Austin, Colorado

The Pretty Young Widow

My grandmother was married twice, first to Benjamin Nodine. When the Civil War broke out, the officers came and took him out of the field to fight for our country. Grandmother said, "He never came to the house but waved his goodbye from the field." Weeks went on and one day a soldier delivered a message to my grand-mother, which told her that her husband had been killed in battle. They had three children. Time went on and my grandmother married the man who had brought the death message to her. He also became my grandfather because later they had three children, one of whom became my mother. Grandfather never tired of telling us the story of his messenger trip to Grandmother's and always added, "When I saw that pretty young widow, I knew I would marry her someday."

Mrs. John Ziegler
Lone Tree, Iowa

Two Terms Of Duty

At the beginning of the Civil War, my maternal grandfather lived near Wilkesbarre, Pennsylvania, and had been married only a short time.

He enlisted on October 16, 1862, in the 177th Pennsylvania regiment and left to serve his country. My grandmother took her baby daughter, who was my mother, and went to live with her parents. My grandfather served his time and came home, but there was a man that didn't want to go. At that time, if one didn't want to go, they could hire another to go in their place. Because Grandfather needed money badly, he accepted the offer of $200 and went again, joining the 198th Pennsylvania volunteers on September 6, 1864, and served until he was discharged at the close of the War. He was never paid the money that was promised.

Two of the battles he was in were the Battle of Gettysburg and the Battle of the Wilderness, but he never liked to talk about war.

He was very sick at one time while in the Army, and couldn't eat. My mother told me that she could remember the day he came home. She was five years old and at school. He came through the schoolyard, picked her up and carried her home on his shoulder.

Because of his sickness, he had brought some of his beans, rice and coffee home with him. He lived to be an old man, but he never ate beans or rice, nor drank another cup of coffee.

H. A. Ives
St. John, Kansas

Bugle And Drum

My father, at the age of 17, enlisted in Company A, 108 Illinois volunteers, and had to say he was 18 in order to enlist. He was the drummer boy the first year, then carried a musket. He was in several battles, and was with the troop that captured Selma, Alabama.

Said when the Rebel band knew they would be captured, they destroyed all their musical instruments. Father was interested in the shell of a snare drum. A youth said to him, "Boss, I know where you can get heads for that," so Father bought the heads, repaired the drum and after coming home he, two of his brothers and a friend or two formed a band that was in demand for all celebrations, picnics and political rallies.

I still have the drum shell and the ebony drum sticks; on the shell is plainly printed "Selma, Alabama."

Father spent six months and eight days in Anderson Prison. Saw the man who was hanged in prison and drank from the spring that broke out on a side hill. Said all the men were so happy to get good water because what they had was so filthy.

Some friends were asking Father about his prison experience. My little girls were just shocked and came to me and asked, "Mamma, what did Grandpa ever do that they put him in prison?"

He used to sing some of his Army songs to us children. I remember part of one.

"When captured by a host of men, each with a loaded gun
They stationed us in an open pen, exposed to rain and sun.
No tents or trees to shelter us, we lay upon the sand
And side by side great numbers died in Dixie's sunny land.
This was our daily bill of fare in this secret saloon
No sugar, tea or coffee there at morning, night or noon,
But a pint of meal, ground cob and all, was served to every man.
For want of fire we ate it raw in Dixie's sunny land."

Mrs. M. D. Warner
Melvern, Kansas

Parental Consent

I will send you a story of my father who was in the Civil War. In 1864 he was only 16 and wanted to enlist. His father was a Baptist circuit rider minister and would not give his consent.

Father told him that if he didn't sign up for him, he would run away and lie about his age. Rather than have his son lie, Grandfather gave his consent.

Father was in the heavy artillery division. He said they were short of ammunition and loaded their cannon with scrap iron or anything they could get in the cannon. Once they put in a log chain, among other things.

He was with Sherman on his March to the Sea. Father was only 17 when the War was over.

The soldiers had the old "cap and ball" revolvers. They had to melt lead and make their own bullets. I have the bullet mold he carried, and it is a prized possession. I still have his songbook with all the Army songs in it. They used to sing around their camp fires at night.

Mrs. J. M. Harvey
Galesburg, Illinois

Shoemaker Inducted Into Service

My grandmother had her husband and seven brothers all in the War at one time. There were 13 children in my grandmother's family, five girls and eight boys.

The youngest boy wanted to go as a drummer boy, but his father set his foot down and would not let him go. They all enlisted from Tarrytown, New York. They were the Van Tassel boys.

My grandfather, John Rowell, was a shoemaker, and the officers came and took him right from his place of business and did not let him come home to tell his family goodbye.

My mother said she slept in a trundle bed, and that night a soldier knocked on the door. When Grandmother went to the door, the soldier told her that Grandfather would not be home as they had taken him to serve in the Army. And my mother said, she could always remember seeing her mother sitting down in a rocking chair and crying her eyes out.

It left Grandmother with five children to raise. She was young as she was only 16 when she was married. But they all came through the War safe.

Grandfather was in the Battle of Bull Run.

Hazel Johnson
Lincoln, Nebraska

New Jersey Infantry Volunteer

William H. Cosgrove served in the Union Army under Sherman during the Civil War. He was enrolled in Co. K, 35th Regiment of New Jersey Infantry Volunteers, 23 September, 1864. His family stayed with relatives in New Jersey during his absence. He was honorably discharged in Washington, D.C., with the rank as private, 30 May 1865. When he applied for a pension in 1890, he stated that he had rheumatism while he was with the troops in Savannah, Georgia, during the winter of 1865. He also complained of heart and kidney disease and dizziness. He was granted a pension of $6 a month.

Information obtained from pension records and family history.

Submitted by Rovilla M. Landry
Kerrville, Texas

Enlisting In Secrecy

After the outbreak of the Civil War, John Ginter, in October 1861, enlisted in Co. G., 5th Kansas Cavalry, having to conduct this movement with great secrecy on account of Rebels being all around him.

The recruiting officer sought him in the wheat field where he was at work, and they agreed to meet at the farmer's house on a certain night. The Lieutenant, however, was obliged to leave before the night appointed for the meeting.

Mr. Ginter's partner swam the Platte River, then got a skiff and by the aid of this, they reached the Missouri River, crossing to Leavenworth, where they joined their regiment. Mr. Ginter was mustered in by General Jim Lane and served three years and two months. He fought at the Battles of Dry Weed, Morriston, Helena, Little Rock, Pine Bluff, Arkansas, and other engagements.

John Ginter was my great-grandfather.

Theresa Stingerie Bainbridge
LaSalle, Colorado

Graybeard Regiment

Dougal McDougal has been long gone, but he is not soon to be forgotten! I am proud to be one of his descendants.

The initials "G.A.R." are clearly visible on his grave marker, indicating that he had been a member of the Grand Army of the Republic with the Union troops during the Civil War. At the age of 54, he became a member of the 37th Infantry from Iowa, made up entirely of volunteers ranging from 50 years to 84 years of age. He served in the 6th Cavalry, Company C (known as the Graybeard Regiment) from 1862 to 1863.

It is our family's understanding that these volunteers were from the northeast Iowa area and were sworn in at McGregor on the Mississippi River. Due to lack of transportation at that time, they were forced to walk to the designated area to be inducted and required to furnish their own weapons and clothing.

He was honorably discharged in 1863 because of an eye infection, which left him legally blind. As a result of his disability, he was granted a monthly pension of $26, which was one of the largest pensions granted.

> Ruth Hill Hager
> Sun City, Arizona

Serving His Adopted Country

My great-grandfather, Joseph A. Roth Sr., felt the call of his adopted country and enlisted for the Civil War. He was in Company C, 96th Illinois Volunteer Infantry, and he served for three years. He was injured and took part in Sherman's March to the Sea. He was discharged in 1865.

Because he was a Civil War veteran, Mr. Roth was entitled to homestead 160 acres instead of 80 acres. He staked out his claim in Lyon County, Iowa. His homestead grant was signed by President Ulysses Grant.

> Submitted by Myrtle May Duin
> George, Iowa

Two Terms At Andersonville

My husband's great-grandfather was a boy when the Civil War broke out. He wanted to go and fight with his older friends and his brother, but he wasn't old enough to enlist. So he ran away and became a drummer boy.

They took him to Andersonville where he was exchanged and then sent home. There he enlisted with the 6th Indiana Cavalry, Co. F. He was captured again and sent to Andersonville where he received an injury from a sword.

Plummers
Osawatomie, Kansas

Runaway Joins The Confederate Army

My great-grandfather's older brother, Marion Dilbeck, was drafted into and fought in the Union Army during the Civil War.

His younger brother, Benson G. Dilbeck, thought he was missing out and ran away and joined the Confederate Army, Company I, 33rd Arkansas Infantry June 24, 1862.

In February 1864, he was given a 10-day furlough. He deserted when his furlough was up. He hid out in the woods in Arkansas until the War ended. He was not punished since he was on the losing side.

Jeneal Riley
Roger, Arkansas

Brother Enlists For Brother

My grandfather was in the Civil War, on the March with Sherman to the Sea. In those days a brother could go for a brother. He was only 14 and had gone for his older brother from New York.

Frances Hoyt Trail
McCook, Nebraska

Away Into The Night

It was back in the year of 1861, that a country boy almost 16 years of age, or rather so young that a razor had never touched the soft down beginning to grow on his face, felt it his duty to enlist and take up arms to help do his bit to preserve the union his country knew, and maybe also because of his Love and Admiration for a tall, tired man down at Washington, the nation's capitol, that was needing the loyal support of his people at a very critical time.

Naturally, the parents of this boy would not give their consent to his enlisting in the Army, saying he was too young to endure the hardships of war and also he was needed at home where a boy of his age was able to do many chores on the farm.

Yet all this talk did not deter him from leaving his home, for one night he packed his few clothes in a small bundle and like the Arab, stole silently away in the darkness. Going to the nearest Army post, Mansfield, Ohio, he enlisted by giving his age as 18, thus making himself two years older than his actual age.

He was just a young country boy, slender of face with dark, curly hair, used to wearing cotton jeans and going barefoot as he pleased, so the Army discipline with the monotony of camp life and his first experience of being away for home for any length of time caused him to become very homesick.

Of course, his parents tried to get him released because he was under age, and also he was needed to help with the work on the farm as his older brother was already serving in their country's service, but he, as well as his parents, was to learn he was in the Army now, and stay, he must.

(Later, the young man saw honorable duty, was captured and served 13 months in prison.)

Isa Palmer
West Salem, Ohio

CHAPTER 3: Battles Of The Blue And The Gray

Captain John C. Smith

Two stories my father told about the Civil War stand out in memory; one was tragic, the other humorous.

Grandfather's family lived in a border state. Most of his family went to the Southern side. When his favorite uncle chose the Northern side, Grandpa, a boy in his teens, soon folowed him into the Union Army.

One battle Grandpa never could erase from his memory was an especially fierce one. After it was over, he was wandering around in a kind of a daze when he heard among the groans of the wounded, a sharp, bitter cry. He went toward the sound and found a man in blue bending over a man in gray. Grandfather looked on in horror while the one in blue gathered the dying boy in gray in his arms. The one in blue was the favorite uncle and the other was the uncle's youngest brother.

Is it any wonder that Grandfather used to say, with a look of pain on his face, " War is always a terrible thing, but Civil War is the most terrible of all."

There was a young man in Grandpa's company by the name of John Smith who thought he was better than other people. When he was made Captain, he was sure of it. Once when they camped near a woods — on a moonlit night — Grandpa awoke and saw a figure stealing towards the woods.

He awakened a buddy and they followed it. Into the woods they went and to a clearing. Evidently the figure thought he was a safe distance from camp for he straightened up and said three times in a commanding voice, "Captain John C. Smith. Law, don't that sound!"

When anyone in our family got a "big head," Grandpa would say with a twinkle in his eye, "Captain John C. Smith. Law, don't that sound!"

Mrs. Grant Larrance
Hutchinson, Kansas

Not Horsin' Around

My father, who enlisted in Indiana in response to Lincoln's second call for volunteers, was 19 years old when he was put on sentry duty to watch out for any approaching enemy while his comrades slept.

It was after a long battle and he was very tired, but contrived to keep awake until 3:30 a.m. Then he was startled by approaching footsteps. At first he could see nothing, but soon discerned a dark figure, which he presumed to be an enemy spy.

According to instructions, he called out, "Who comes there?" There was no reply, but the figure came nearer. He repeated the call and still there was no answer. Then came the critical moment. His instructions were to call out those three words three times, and then if no reply was forthcoming, he was to shoot to kill. Terror seized him. "I cannot kill a man!" he cried and prayed. He would himself be shot at sunrise if he disobeyed the order.

The third time he screamed the words and prepared to shoot, and in that instant, the figure came closer to him. He saw it was a horse.

Father said it was for him the happiest incident of the entire Civil War.

Mrs. N. E. Belanger
East Orange, New Jersey

20-20 Vision

The most serious thing my father had to do in the War was when he substituted for his bunk pal who was too sick to do guard duty. Father had done his guard duty and undertook his pal's guard duty following, and it was hard to keep awake so many nights. If the head officer caught you asleep while on guard duty, he was supposed to shoot you. My father rubbed strong tobacco juice in his eyes to keep awake.

In later years my father almost lost his eyesight.

Clara Jackson
Corning,Iowa

A Happy Reunion

On a day in April, at the very beginning of the Civil War, Grandfather and his brother left their homes and families to do their part in the terrible struggle, having the great good fortune to be assigned to the same outfit.

That morning the order came to capture Mission Ridge. In order to bolster their own and each other's courage as they pushed their way up the slope in withering fire, the men set up a fierce hollering and yelling.

Suddenly Grandfather was down, and unable to get up again, as his comrades kept on until the hill was theirs. Then he discovered a bullet had pierced his leg. He always claimed he never knew, in all the excitement, when he was hit. It was loss of blood that downed him.

Later in the day, lying there dazed with pain, Grandfather noticed a man down below moving slowly from fallen body to body, now and then turning one carefully as if seeking to find a certain person. This went on for hours, or so it seemed to the suffering man, until suddenly the searcher came near enough for recognition. Yes, it was his own beloved brother! And you can imagine that reunion! Neither were ever ashamed of those tears!

Mae T. McCaw
Hemet, California

Prayers Comfort Wounded

This story about my grandfather was told us by a man who had been an observer.

A man had been wounded and was dying. He asked the Captain to pray for him before he died. The Captain felt unfit to pray and asked his company, "Can any of you men pray with this man?" No one volunteered.

Then a man spoke up, "There is a man over in Company F who can pray for him."

"Go get him," ordered the Captain.

The soldier soon returned, accompanied by the man of whom he had spoken. He knelt by the dying soldier and prayed. The soldiers and Captain listened with tears in their eyes as the dying man, comforted, died in the arms of the one who had prayed for him.

The Captain thanked the good man, and he returned to his company where he was an orderly.

The man from Company F, Ohio, was my grandfather, James Garnet Thornton. He had been a Christian since he was 17 years of age. He was soon relieved of carrying a gun and fighting and was put in charge of caring for the wounded in the field first aid stations and later in the Army hospital.

Probably he prayed with many other boys who were dying. He never told us much about it.

Iva Thornton Locke
Portsmouth, Ohio

Proud Of Eagle Mascot

My grandfather was a Civil War volunteer, having answered Lincoln's first call. He told us about this incident in the War.

In the first part of 1861 in the Civil War, the 8th Wisconsin regiment was at Belmont, Missouri, where they found an eagle's nest. Some of them cut the tree and captured one, which had a broken wing. They called him Abe.

The soldiers fed and cared for the eagle. One soldier was paid to carry the eagle on a perch. The perch had a wooden shield painted with stars and stripes like the flag, and it was carried by a long handle.

When the eagle was hungry, it would fly away to eat and then fly back to its perch. Grandpa saw it do this.

The eagle was wounded sometimes, but always got well. The day Vicksburg surrendered, the eagle flopped his wings and screamed all day, while the army marched and the band played.

Abe was cared for until he died. Then his body was mounted and is in the museum at Washington, D.C.

Mildred Gladden
Bloomfield, Missouri

Excerpts From Letter Written Home By Benjiman Lewis

April 15, 1863
Aboard the Bobray
Alexander, Louisiana

"Have had one of the hottest times since I have been in the Army. You probably heard about Banks' defeat by land and river. We was with the fleet. We got about 500 miles up Red River when Banks fell back, and the Rebs cut off our rear and got on our rear with their artillery. We had to run their battery for 200 miles. Our company was on board the Bobray, loaded with ammunition. She had five shells through her and musket balls without number. None of our Company was hurt, but five Battery men were wounded. It seemed that they were bound to take our fleet, but our gun battery made them hunt their holes.

April 16

We will probably leave here today for Granitco up the river 90 miles, where our Regiment is. Banks has fell back there and is raring to go again. (Benjiman G. Lewis's two-year-old daughter, whom he had never seen, died while he was on this mission.)

45

We were in a pretty tight place but got out all right. We ran four batteries and landed at dark at Cante. As we came near shore, we could see lines of men four deep. We thought they were Rebs and fired into them from the boat, then found they were General Smith's from 17th Army Corp. come to help us, but so dark we couldn't see.

General Banks has lost lots of men — they say 4,000.

July 15, 1863

We left Vixburg the 5th of this month to chase old Johnson. We chased him here at Jackson, Mississippi, and are fighting him on all sides. Our brigade was ordered forward to charge the fortifications, which we did — the 3rd Iowa, 41st Illinois, 8th Illinois and 33rd Wisconsin, which is our regiment.

Our regiment did not charge, for we did not get there in time. We was on the extreme right, so we had farther to go through brush. The other regiments charged and was cut to pieces and had to fall back with great slaughter.

Our regiment fell back by order of General Lawman. Other regiments lost 400 men killed, wounded and taken prisoner. General Lawman is under arrest and was sent to trial for making that charge and not knowing where and how many he charged against, and for sending his men into a trap.

Ours charged against five Rebel brigades that were behind forts. The 3rd Iowa stayed until they were cut to pieces. Their Colonel killed. A shell struck him first and knocked him out of his saddle. He got on his horse and ordered his men forward and got a musket ball in his neck.

Don't know how long it will take to whip the Rebs at Jackson. Old Johnson is more of a fighter than Pemberton. He has about 40,000 men. We had a very hard march getting here from Vixburg. So hot and we have such loads to carry and hot woolen pants and shirts.

The Rebs surrendered on the 4th of July. We really celebrated, but had orders to be ready to march at any moment with four days rations and our haversacks.

Oct. 5, 1864
Cape Girardeau

We arrived here last night on the Mississippi River, 40 miles above Cairo, after a fatiguing march of 325 miles. Have been after Old Price but did not see him. Our supplies have run out and we have no tents. We are under the command of General Mowery, an old tyrant.

I went to a house this morning to get a warm breakfast of biscuits and butter. Cost me 25 cents. I was on half rations on our march of 19 days — 325 miles through swamps, mud, rain and rivers.

Oct. 17, 1865

Jut in Nashville — Matt in Chattanooga in big fight. (Jut and Matt were brothers of Benjiman Lewis.)

Camped at Hollersprings, Mississippi, where our General surrendered up the place without firing a shot, with 2,000 men. He was sent home in disgrace."

Lianne McNeil
Aloha, Oregon

Diary Of Battles

My grandfather was in the Civil War, and I have a diary he kept during the time. He was in an Ohio regiment.

On Aug 23, 1862, he wrote, "Went through Washington City."

24th, "Got out of cars at Washington Station."

26th, "Went to guard General Pope's headquarters."

27th, "Went to battleground that evening, the wounded still on the field, stayed on the field all night, buried the dead, then went to Bull Run."

Sept 17th, "Battle of Antietam."

Oct 3, "Visited by the President."

June 5, 1863, "Went to Liberty where we joined Col. Wilders's force of mounted infantry."

June 6, "Left Liberty and started to Murfeesboro."

June 24th, "Rained hard all day and all night, continued artillery fire."

June 25th, "Stayed on the line all day and all night."

28th, "General Rosencrans came in."

July 5, "Stayed in camp and drew a part of day's rations."

8th, "Drew one day's ration of bread and coffee."

Sept 5, "Went to Trenton, Georgia."

Sept 11, "Went across Lookout Mountain and drove in the Rebel pickets."

Sept 17, "Firing commenced early in the morning and we were ordered to the front. Firing was kept up all day."

Sept 19, "Battle of Chickamauga, Col. James wounded, and Maj. Adney and two Lieut. Wm. Ross of our company died."

Sept 20, "Second day of battle, Harrison Howel killed."

Sept 22, "Stayed ready for battle all day and commenced to fortify at night."

23rd, "Worked on the fortifications nearly all day."

24th, "Went out to reconnoiter the enemy's position, had a heavy skirmish, heavy firing until 10 o'clock."

Oct 13, "Election Day, 43 votes."

Oct 21, "General Rosecrans left us; General Thomas took over."

Dessie Cassity
Stratton, Colorado

The Surrender Of General Lee

My father was a Civil War veteran, having served in Company C, 12th Ohio Cavalry, for 19 months, being transferred at Knoxville, Tennessee, to the 129th Ohio Infantry, serving eight months during which time he marched with Sherman to the sea.

He helped fight the last battle, the Battle of Gettysburg. It was a bloody, three-day battle. He said the morning of the surrender that Lee's men charged on them early while they were eating breakfast, killing several of their men.

They hurriedly packed their canteens and got ready for a big battle. When General Lee rode up on the hill on a white horse and run up the white flag, thus surrendering to General Grant, he said cheers of joy went up. They had won a great victory. He was honorably discharged at the close of the War.

Mrs. John Rigg
Lenora, Kansas

Cool Milk In The Springhouse Trough

My father moved to my grandfather's farm which was located about three miles from a small town, Silver Run, Maryland. It is located on one of the main highways leading from Baltimore and to Gettysburg, Pennsylvania, where the last battle of the Civil War was fought.

My grandmother often told one story of their experiences in those days. They had started to build a new brick house and my mother was a baby at that time. My grandfather's farm was located in Maryland, but was close to the Pennsylvania line. It was about 16 miles to Gettysburg from where we lived.

My grandmother told me they could hear the noise from the battlefield very good, and the noise from the cannons and guns was terrific. My grandmother told how the soldiers came through on horseback, passed their home, jumped the horses over fences and gates, made a tour of the buildings and went to the springhouse.

The springhouse was built right by a large spring and was so arranged with a wooden trough built in the house so the water from the spring ran in one end of the trough and out the other end.

The milk was kept in stone jars in the springhouse trough. The soldiers drank all the milk and took anything else they could find to eat. Grandmother said the place sure looked a wreck after they had left.

Mrs. General Montgomery
Lebanon, Missouri

Oysters Alive

At the outbreak of the Civil War my grandfather Frank, then 19, and his two younger brothers Jimmie, 16, and Tommy, 15, all marched away to war, joining the Missouri Infantry (Union side).

The middle boy, Jimmie, fell in the siege of Vicksburg and Tommy later died of malaria somewhere in the South while Grandfather continued on and joined Sherman's March to the Sea. He became very ill with cholera on the March, and each mile he thought would be his last. But with a burning determination to reach the seaside, he stumbled on with his company until their destination was reached.

He laid in the sunshine on the Georgia beach and ate nothing for days except raw oysters and seafood which were within his reach. As if by miracle, he recovered and rejoined his company.

Before the close of the War he became a Second Lieutenant and led in the capture of the famous outlaw bushwhacker Marmaduke.

I often think that I owe my chance to be here to that humble little seafood, the oyster.

Mrs. Oscar Stamm
Washington, Kansas

Proud To Be G.A.R.

My father was Edmund N. Creekmur, Late Private, Company K, 49th Regiment, Illinois Volunteers. He was born Jan. 8, 1846, and died Nov. 4, 1914. While in the service he was shot through the right hip. He had to do so much marching that the flesh wore off of the ends of his toes, to the bones, but his hip injury caused him to suffer at times and limp the rest of his life. He was always proud that he belonged to the Grand Army of the Republic, and I am, too.

Mrs. J. P. Lawson
Salem, Illinois

Hot Foot

My husband's grandfather served in the Iowa Infantry during the Civil War and his experience was no tragedy, except to him. He always complained about walking all over the South and said he knew every foot of ground between Little Rock and Mobile. His company never did come in contact with the enemy and the only wound he suffered was when he stepped in a kettle of hot soup one night which a "blankety blank fool" set too far from the fire.

Mrs. Morris Doty
Missouri Valley, Iowa

Water Provides Temporary Peace

Northwest Missouri saw several skirmishes during the Civil War, altho there was not the bitterness found in more southerly places. Near my grandmother's home was a never-failing, hand-dug well, walled up with the native limestone that was so plentiful in the region. A good supply of water was hard to find during those hot summer months, so the Boys in Blue and the Boys in Gray declared a daily truce at sunset when not a shot was fired.

The first evening the Southern troops came first to the well, dipped water for their horses and drew a supply for their personal needs, after which they withdrew a reasonable distance so the Northern troops could do the same. The next evening the order was reversed and the Northern troops drew water first. Older people here could remember when the sound of guns ceased at sunset.

This well was still in existence when the farm came into my possession. A few years later a state road was built which took the famous old well. Even now, however, when evening comes and peaceful quiet settles in our valley, it is not hard to imagine the ghostly figures in blue and gray gathered about the old well.

Mrs. Curtis Seal
Denver, Missouri

The Bible Of Dunker Church

In the Civil War days General Robert E. Lee pitched camp a week nearby at the Longmeadow North of Hagerstown, Maryland, in 1863, and notified the people in the community that his headquarters would be in the Dunker Church.

Ann Rowland was the first visitor General Lee had, and she called on him to hand over the pulpit Bible to her. The General arose from his desk where he was engaged in writing and stood for a few moments in silence. A rare personality was standing in his presence, and with great admiration and courtesy, General Lee said, "Mrs. Rowland, we use this Bible in our morning worship. If it is left here I pledge my honor that the Holy Word shall be kept safely, and no harm will come to the place of worship." We still have the Bible.

The battle scarred the church. The Battle of South Mountain in Maryland during the Civil War took place on a Sunday, September 14, 1863. A crowd assembled at a historic spot for worship, the Mumma Church overlooking Antietam and Sharpsburg. All was peaceful, and they made their way home, not realizing what would come tomorrow.

In the afternoon children at play saw smoke and heard the roar of guns on South Mountain. The battle had begun with fury in the early afternoon.

Both armies were concentrating all day Monday. Tuesday skirmishing continued. Wednesday morning before daybreak the battle began with fury. The line swayed back and forth. Soon the Mummet home, bar and building were on fire.

General Hooker, who commanded, threw the whole division into attack, and came up the slope where the Dunker Church stood, was battered with shot and shells.

Battered, bloodstained and broken walls still stood. It was used for a hospital during the battle.

The Bible was carried away by two soldiers of the 107th New York Regiment and kept as a souvenir. At a reunion in Elmira, New York, it became known that the widow of a soldier had the

Bible in her possession. Money was raised, the book purchased and put into the hands of John T. Lewis to return it to the church at Sharpsburg.

Mrs. Ezra A. Petie
Hagerstown, Maryland

The Battle Of Wilson Creek

Aunt Nan loved to tell her version of the Battle of Wilson Creek. "I remember August 10, 1861," she'd begin. "Early that morning as I did my chores, I heard a steady rumble like thunder coming from the south.

"Hey, Sis!" I yelled. "There's a storm coming. There's a dark cloud south of town and thunder like a thousand wagons. Help me get the chores done before it rains."

The thunder continued to rumble and the clouds continued to hang low in the south. Right after noon, a neighbor brought news. "There's a big battle raging south of Springfield, near the Old Wire Road on those wooded hills on Wilson Creek! Runners say them Rebels are cutting our Army like hailstones cut ripe wheat!"

Aunt Nan always paused in her story at this point before saying, "All day we listened to the horrible cannon thunder. We watched the horrible rolling cloud that hovered over the southern horizon with fear in our hearts. We prayed for our men, our neighbors and our Army.

"News came slowly in those days, but day-by-day and bit-by-bit we heard the bloody battle story; about friends and neighbors killed and wounded. We heard of the death of our General Lyon and the retreat of the Federal Army toward St. Louis."

Grammy always finished this story the same way, "War is a horrible thing! One of the bloodiest battles of all times was that Battle of Wilson Creek."

Mamie Fly
Wichita, Kansas

The Battle Of Kirksville

I have heard Uncle Tim tell many times that during the Civil War he remembers that he was just a small boy. He was with his father in the top of the courthouse at Kirksville, Missouri, when the Rebels tried to capture that town. During the hot fighting his father took the boy and slipped out to their team, climbed into the wagon and drove north of town, dodging bodies of dead fighting men on the way. After leaving the boy with some friends living north of Kirksville, the father returned to Kirksville and saw the Confederates driven off. That was what is known as the Battle of Kirksville.

Velma Partin
Unionville, Missouri

Lee's Lost Order

A scrap of paper found 137 years ago by a Bloomfield, Indiana, soldier may have turned the fortunes of battle to the North's advantage in America's Civil War of 1861-1865.

Soldiers of the 27th Indiana Volunteers Regiment were checking a Maryland bivouac site September 13, 1862, when Corporal Barton W. Mitchell found Special Order No. 191 detailing movements and battle plans of the Confederate Army. The order, wrapped around three cigars, had been written by General Robert E. Lee and was intended only for the eyes of his most trusted Confederate officers.

Mitchell had enlisted in the army at Bloomfield in the summer of 1861 and then was sent to Indianapolis where the 27th Regiment had been formed. When Mitchell found the lost order, he and First Sgt. John M. Bloss, of Muncie, the ranking "non-com" of Company F, turned the paper over to Colonel Silas Colgrove, who immediately dispatched the information to Federal Army headquarters.

Four days later, September 17, 1862, Union forces under General George B. McClellan clashed with Lee's Army of Northern Virginia near the town of Sharpsburg, Maryland.

The resulting Battle of Antietam, named for the creek near the town, marked the "bloodiest" single day of war in American history. When night came, Federal losses totaled 12,410. Southern casualties numbered 10,700.

The 46-year-old Mitchell sustained serious wounds at Antietam, submitting to medical treatment for eight months. The Greene County soldier was out of the hospital in time to rejoin the 27th Indiana Regiment for the Battle of Gettysburg, Pennsylvania, July 1-3, 1863.

The finding of Special Order No. 191 was significant, but in trying to assess its impact on the outcome of Antietam, and particularly the entire War, historians have left a number of questions unanswered.

In fact, historians differ as to whether the lost order worked to the benefit of the North, or if, strangely enough, gave Lee's Southern Army the advantage at Antietam. Full knowledge of the movements of Lee's troops and battle strategy caused the cautious McClellan to take three days to prepare for battle, rather than pressing the South before Lee was ready to fight. Methodically, McClellan placed men, guns and back-up troops into battle position, and then insisted on making a personal inspection.

While McClellan dallied, General Lee wisely used the time to re-establish battle lines and bring in reinforcements. General Thomas (Stonewall) Jackson had captured the arsenal at Harper's Ferry, West Virginia, taking 13,000 arms, 49 field guns and 24 mountain howitzers. A 15-mile march to the north brought Jackson's troops to a link up by September 16 with Lee's forces in the Sharpsburg, Maryland, area.

Although the lost order intelligence did not give the strength of Lee's army, McClellan "knew" he was going to meet a superior force and took the better part of three days to prepare for battle. Actually, McClellan's 87,000-man striking force outnumbered the Confederate forces more than two to one. Lee had only about 41,000. McClellan thought Lee had at least 120,000 men at Antietam.

While the North won the battle, McClellan's procrastination allowed Lee's army to escape back to the safety of Virginia. The North's failure to press the battle when fighting ended September 17th afforded the defeated Confederates time to splash across the shallow Potomac River, almost at leisure.

In early November, 1862, about six weeks after Antietam, President Lincoln dismissed McClellan as commander of the Northern Armies. A perfectionist who never took calculated risks, "Little Mac" never realized his full potential as a field general. Lincoln often said he had the "slows." The War dragged on for nearly three more years before the South surrendered at Appomattox in April, 1865.

General Lee's foray into the North was aimed at carrying the brunt of the war to the enemy. Until Antietam, the long shadow of war had fallen across southern soil. Feeling triumphant after the South's victories at Bull Run and Manassas in the first year of the War, Lee crossed the Potomac into Maryland. Stonewall Jackson had moved against the arsenal at Harper's Ferry and would then link up with Lee's forces to start a concerted drive toward Washington, D.C.

The design of Lee's move would be a two-pronged attack to the east, seizing Harrisburg, Pennsylvania, then the principal railroad hub of the North, and pressing on toward Washington. With Washington in its possession, the South figured the War would be won.

Reportedly, four copies of Special Order No. 191 were made, each in General Lee's handwriting. One copy was marked for General D. H. Hill. The lost order was found in the bivouac area just outside Frederick, Maryland, where units of Hill's Corps had encamped a few days before. In later years, Hill denied he ever received the order.

Before his death in 1870, five years after the War ended, Lee attributed the wrecking of his plans solely to the lost order. McClellan also said after the War he believed the intelligence order helped the North to win the Battle of Antietam. Hill would remark in later years that the "losing of the dispatch was the saving of Lee's Army." McClellan's halting commitment of units and subsequent failure to capitalize on the advantage may have swept away opportunities to end the War in 1862.

Mitchell was never rewarded for his finding of the order. Years later, McClellan recalled the incident and stated the soldier should be honored, but the General could not recall Mitchell's name.

Samuel D. Heaton
Indianapolis, Indiana

Find My Wife And Marry Her

The Childreth family history begins with Andrew Jackson Childreth (Jack as he was always known).

When a young man, Jack Childreth enlisted in the Civil War, and he was in the 52nd Regiment from Illinois as a Confederate. While in the Civil War, he and another young man by the last name of Owen became real buddies. The young man had to leave his bride of a short time when he was drafted. She was pregnant, and he talked and worried about her and the coming child.

The two men fought side-by-side, and Mr. Owen was mortally wounded. When he was dying, he asked Jack Childreth to find his wife when the War was over and marry her, if she consented. Jack agreed, and did just that. Her name was Paralee Jenkins Owen, and the baby was named Lizzie.

Julia Oleeta Childreth Bolinger
Pretty Prairie, Kansas

Second Funeral 66 Years Later

When I was a child, there were several elderly Civil War veterans in our small town of Coleridge, Nebraska. The one I remember best was Lewis Dennis.

In August 1861, Mr. Dennis, a Union soldier in the Civil War, was wounded in the hip and left for dead on the field of battle.

57

Later, he was taken to a Confederate hospital, where after recovery, he was paroled, not to take up arms against the Confederacy.

At this time his folks at home received official notice of his death and held his funeral, believing the body had been buried with hundreds of others near the scene of battle.

After the War, Mr. Dennis came home. He died April, 1929. His second funeral was preached 66 years after his first.

This story was an entry for Robert L. Ripley's second edition of *Believe It Or Not Book.*

Clarice Morrison
Colridge, Nebraska

A Civil War Song

Wounded and bleeding upon the field
Two dying soldiers lay.
One thought of Mother at home alone
Feeble, old and gray.
One of the sweetheart he left in town
Happy, young and gay.
One kissed a ringlet of thin gray hair,
One kissed a lock of brown.
They closed their eyes to the earth and skies
Just as the sun went down.

Ruth Jincks
Bethany, Missouri

Terrible Toll At Opequan Creek

The 28th Iowa fought in the "Bloody Angle" at Opequan and lost nearly 100 in killed and wounded. Company G, to which the writer belonged, lost 13 men — five being killed on the field, one mortally wounded, five severely wounded and two slightly wounded — and this out of a total of 33 that were in the engagement. The Battle of Opequan Creek, east of Winchester, Virginia, was fought September 19, 1864.   Excerpts from "Old Glory At Opequan" follow.

> In Dixie's land our Hawkeye band then dared
> The hosts of "Southern chivalry;"
> Good men and true, and brave ones too, there bared
> Their arms for death or victory,
> And sternly fought and nobly wrought
> On the storm-swept field of Opequan,
> Where Early's hosts rushed madly on
> To where we rallied in the wood
> Around Old Glory there.
>
> This too we claim, that never shame our record
> Bold and fair and clean shall mar;
> Ever we'll strive to keep alive the spirit
> That prevailed in days of yore,
> When comrades fell mid shout and yell
> On sod red-stained with crimson gore,
> Where furious raged the fiery fray
> On that eventful autumn day,
> When thick as leaves our comrades lay
> Around Old Glory there.

Ruby Zabel
Daykin, Nebraska

Valiant Effort

My grandfather, Ransom Varney, joined the Civil War from New York State, the 30th Regiment, Company G. He served until 1864. One incident that I remember him telling about happened during the Battle of Chancellorsville. The flag bearer was shot down. Grandfather picked up the flag and carried it throughout the battle, which they lost.

Anona McConaghy
Bellflower, California

A Gallant Defender

A yellowed portrait of a slender old man caught my attention today. His keen eye is squinting down the long barrel of a flintlock rifle.

That man was my great-grandfather who served in the Civil War. He enlisted a month after fighting began and did not muster out until a few weeks after the last shot was fired. In the photo he is barefooted as was always his custom in summer, pant legs rolled up enough to keep them out of dust or mud.

The rest of Grandpa's life, he reminisced about his war experiences to anyone who would listen. He never tired of telling how he served as a forager, gathering food from the countryside for his comrades, as they pushed into new territory. His captain admitted that Grandpa had his eccentricities, but said, "The nation has no more gallant defender."

Grandpa's captain told how Grandpa refused to leave an injured comrade when the regiment was ordered to fall back. The captain saw at a glance that the wounded man must be left behind. Grandpa declared, with tears streaming down his face, that he would die first.

Only by hard coaxing was Grandpa persuaded he must escape in order to further serve his country. By hard running, he did escape into the woods with the rest of the men. The next day, the wounded boy was found dead, kindly placed under a tree by a soldier in the opposing army. He had been made as comfortable as possible, with his knapsack under his head, canteen of water within reach.

From an article originally printed in *Capper's*, November 7, 1989.

Submitted by Elaine Carr
Nyssa, Oregon

Lee And Grant Ride To Appomattox

My paternal grandpa, Joshua Tecumseh Kirby, born 1843, lied of his age to join in the great American adventure when recruiters signed him into Co. G., 76th Ill. Inf. under Grant. It cited service at the siege of Vicksburg, battles at Jackson's Crossroads, Champion Hill and siege and assult at Fort Blakely, Alabama.

My dad said Grandpa saw General Lee riding his horse to surrender at Appomattox, every inch a distinguished figure. Grant followed in unkempt attire.

Emmett Kirby
Champaign, Illinois

Settler Arrives In Time To Become Soldier

I would sit in my little rocking chair beside my grandfather, rocking and listening to these stories.

My grandparents left Indiana with two small children in a Covered Wagon, traveling for days before reaching what is now Kansas, to stake the Claim of 160 Acres of free land. This land was only two miles from the Mo. line, which had joined the Union as a slave State.

On arriving in Linn County, the friends that had reached Kansas sometime before met them several miles from the place they planned to call Home. Told Grandfather to work fast, get the wife and two Children to hide in a cornfield and take one horse and move west as fast as he could to where the Union Soldiers Camp was. The friends helped unload the Wagon, Took the other horse to wooded area, where it was tied to a tree, the wagon was placed in tall grass. This had to be done to keep the bushwhackers from Mo. from stealing them. If they had met Grandfather before he reached Union Camp, he would have been shot.

The Word had reached the Union Camp in Linn Co. That Price (General) in the Southern Army Was Planning to move across Eastern Kansas and reach Fort Scott. The Union Army had a big supply of guns, also their trained men was in camp there.

Camped close to Mound City, Kansas, most of these men was untrained, and had only hoped to be farmers. When the Raiders moved into Linn Co. they got a big surprise, these men fought as the South had never seen before. What men that had not been killed, gave up within a few days. This was a great Victory for the Union Army.

My grandfather was shot in the leg; he could not walk, no way to stop the bleeding. He crawled two miles away from the battle-field, passed out and was finally picked up by men of the North and taken to a makeshift hospital in Mound City.

Where Grandmother and the little children were hiding in the cornfield, this was only a few miles from where the fighting was taking place. They could hear the guns, also one night there was some men on horses rode around this cornfield hunting for people and whatever they could steal.

Grandmother had the family dog. She and the children talked to the dog, prayed it would not bark and give their hiding place away.

The second night in the cornfield, a light rain came, their bedding was cold and wet for the rest of their stay in the cornfield.

When word came to Grandmother the battle was over; however, Grandfather had been shot and could be dead.

Grandmother and a friend started walking with buckets of water to try and find him. As they walked across this field it was covered with blood, dead and dying men from both sides. Grand-mother said she gave every man that was still alive on the ground a drink. After walking five miles, their water was gone. They met some Union soldiers, that was checking the field for their men, told her Grandfather had been found and was in the hospital.

Grandmother went back to the children and friends, looked for their horse and wagon, they had not been found. The horse Grandfather had rode away to battle was killed.

When Grandfather returned home to start their new life on free Kansas soil, they both thanked God. Their hardships had meant freedom for everyone.

Evelyn Hamilton
Pleasanton, Kansas

Mother Nature Saves Wounded Soldier

I don't have any personal stories of the Civil War, but a close friend of mine, now dead, had a story that needs to be told. This friend's grandfather had come from Germany only a short time earlier, but that did not keep him from fighting to preserve his new country.

In one terrible battle he was wounded and left on the battlefield for days — long enough for maggots to hatch from the eggs the flies laid in his wounds, especially those in one leg. If that hadn't happened — that the maggots ate the rotting flesh, he surely would have died. When he was found and taken in for treatment, the attending surgeon planned to saw off the wounded leg, but the owner begged and pled that he not do it, even to promising him some fine cows he owned in Germany if the leg was spared. Surprisingly, the leg was saved along with its owner's life. Although the surgeon kidded this ex-German about his new cows, they never reached America.

Marjorie Crouch
Uvalde, Texas

Invasion Of Kentucky

During the summer of 1862, Confederate troops had been forced south from President Abraham Lincoln's home state of Kentucky. The two closest Rebel armies were in Tennessee. The commanders of those two Armies, Generals Kirby Smith and Braxton Bragg, were determined to regain a hold in the state, knowing what a crushing blow it would be to the North.

Believing that Kentuckians would rally to support their forces, the two Confederate Armies invaded Kentucky. General Bragg's forces by-passed the Union Army near Nashville and headed toward Louisville where they intended to capture federal supplies.

When Bragg discovered the Union Army, led by Don Carlos Buell, pursued them, he turned toward Bardstown, going into an area known as Muldraugh's Hill in LaRue

County, past the small cabin on Knob Creek where Abraham Lincoln lived as a boy.

Hiding near the road in some bushes, watching the Confederates advance, was 16-year-old George Powell, my great-grandfather. A year later, George enlisted in the Union Army. (While on picket duty, he became ill, having caught the measles. He received an honorable discharge, but his eyesight suffered the rest of his life because of this disease.)

When the Union and Confederate Armies met at the small town of Perryville just outside Bardstown on the afternoon of October 8, 1862, it appeared that the Confederates would win easily. However, 40,000 fresh Union soldiers were readying for attack, and the Confederates were forced to retreat. The Battle of Perryville was a downward turning point for the Confederate Army. They never again pushed so far north.

Linda Powell Parker
Buffalo, Kentucky

Battle Of Lexington

The Battle of Lexington (Missouri) was one of the strangest of the Civil War. The Federals could have ferried the river, but waited too long. The Guards could have closed in sooner, but had no gun caps, and for a week they waited.

On Wednesday morning, September 19, 1861, the Confederates had the town encircled with an iron ring. Bledsoe's battery under the command of Captain Emmett MacDonald while Bledsoe was recovering from his wound, was posted in front of Major A. G. Young's house. Farther out, another ring of reserves surrounded the town, and many more waited at the fairground.

Finally, the ammunition wagons arrived, and couriers arrived on winded horses from Arkansas with satchels of gun caps. The Confederate band had been sidetracked at Macpelah Cemetery, so the clear penetrating roar of "Old Sacramento" filled the air as the curtain went up, and the battle began, not for slavery, nor for secession, but for invasion.

Between the works and the orchard at Anderson's house, the Federals, commanded by Colonel James A. Mulligab, had sniper pits filled with riflemen. These were driven back and the house was taken over at noon that September 18th. Then in mid-afternoon the Federals made a terrific assault and after a heavy death toll, the house was recaptured.

A company from Colonel Hughs's regiment had captured the Federal boats, one of which was loaded with valuable stores. Meanwhile, General McBride's and General Harris's divisions had stormed and occupied the bluff north of Anderson house, which enabled them to harrass the Federals and pin them down.

The Federals couldn't get out, nor could they get any relief from the outside. Their food was low, their water was gone, their ammunition was exhausted, and the stench from dead horses was terrible. They'd dug a well 90 feet deep, but to no avail, so they filled it with dead horses. Sharp-shooters picked off anyone who exposed themselves, and thirst-crazed horses were plunging out of control. The Federals shot many of their fine horses rather than let them fall into enemy hands.

Before sundown, the Guards under Harris came up behind a large barricade of wet hemp bales which they rolled forward and with assistance from the bluff above, the Anderson house was recaptured. The battle raged on until Friday, 20th. Bledsoe was back in action and commanding his battery from a rocking chair. About 2 p.m. the Federals ran out of ammunition, and one of Mulligan's men, without his permission, ran up a white flag of surrender.

At 3:00 an orderly came bearing a flag of truce from General Price and a note asking why the firing had ceased. Colonel Mulligan sent back a reply, saying: "General, I hardly know, unless you've surrendered." After General Price assured him that he hadn't surrendered, Mulligan learned that after running out of ammunition his troops had raised the white flag, so he had no choice but to surrender.

General Price moved his headquarters into Anderson's yard and in a roped-off circle under a tree, the surrender was accomplished.

Kathryn D. Clausen
De Land, Florida

Bullet Memento

I had two great-grandfathers participate in the Civil War. You might say they characterized the beginning and the end of the conflict.

Great-grandpa Joseph Baughman joined the 105th Pennsylvania Volunteers Infantry shortly after the first Battle of Manasses. From that time forward, his unit participated in every campaign and major battle, except Antietam, that took place in the eastern states.

At Gettysburg, his unit was stationed near the Peach Orchard at the start of the second day of the battle. They were overrun by the Confederates and retreated past Devil's Den and through the Wheat Field, taking up defensive positions on the slopes of Cemetery Ridge. Here they held off the Confederates trying to take the ridge.

In 1864 at the Battle of North Anna River, Grandpa was wounded in the leg, while trying to establish a bridgehead across the river. He spent the remainder of the War convalescing in a hospital in Washington, D. C. His unit fought on through the War, being at Appomattox when General Lee surrendered. The family still retains the bullet that was removed from his leg.

My great-grandpa Henry Murry joined the 194th Ohio Infantry, just a month or so before the end of the War. As he was too young to volunteer freely, his father signed a release for him. One night when his unit was on maneuvers, they bivouacked in a church cemetery. Henry was rather apprehensive about sleeping with the dead. An older, battle-experienced veteran told him, "You might as well get used to it, son, where we are going you

won't be sleeping over them, you will be sleeping beside them."
Luckily, the War was over before they reached the battlefront, and
their unit was mustered out.

Ivan L. Pfalser
Caney, Kansas

Battle Of Champion Hill

Living now in this land of plenty, it's next to impossible to turn
back the pages to the terrible Civil War when no one could be sure
this great nation would survive.

Brig. Gen. John A. Logan's 31st regiment of Illinois volunteers,
of which my grandpa John Brandon was an eager participant, did
their state (yes, their whole country) proud from almost the onset
of the War Between the States. The men of the 31st slung their
knapsacks and lay on the high ground looking across to Champion
Hill farmhouse where enemy field batteries were positioned to
defend the double line of infantry.

A Corporal Anderson of a Missouri brigade later told Herb
Phillips, author of *Champion Hill*, of seeing Southern ladies on the
lawn of the Roberts's house nearby singing "Dixie" and cheering
their men on.

Logan rode up, proud and straight in the saddle and pronounced,
"We are about to fight the battle for Vicksburg." The order — "Fix
bayonets" was quickly followed by "Forward — double quick —
march!" His men rose up, plunged into the deep underbrush and
soon faced the enemy at close range. A Corporal (later Capt.)
Byers of Iowa wrote: "I have been in (what history pronounced)
greater battles than Champion Hill, but only this once did I see two
lines of blue and gray stand close together and fire into each
other's faces for an hour and a half! I think the courage of
the private soldier on that awful day gave us Vicksburg, made
Grant immortal and helped save this country."

Norman Diefenbach
Harrisburg, Illinois

Bullet In the Knee

My grandfather, John William, was in the Battle of Shiloh and was injured — a bullet in the knee. Prisoner for 11 months, Andersonville prison. He was released back to Missouri. He had the bullet in his knee at the end of the War. I believe he died with the bullet in his knee.

Myrtle Winsor
Burns, Kansas

Gunboats On The Western Rivers

Journalist Charles Carleton Coffin includes in my treasured heirloom book a chapter entitled "The Capture of Fort Henry." His descriptive detail, as well as the military movements, provide an unforgettable picture.

The Confederate States Army erected two forts on the northern line of Tennessee, one on the Tennessee River (Ft. Henry), another on the Cumberland River, to prevent Union troops from reaching the heart of the Confederacy via water.

The Union realized that "a fleet of gunboats would be needed on the Western rivers, and Captain Andrew H. Foote of the Navy was placed in charge of their construction. They were built in Cincinnati and St. Louis, and taken to Cairo (Illinois), where they received their crews, armament and outfit."

Writer Coffin gives a picturesque account of Cairo of that day. "(Cairo) is a modern town of several thousand inhabitants on the tongue of land at the mouth of the Ohio. Let us look at the place as it appeared on the first day of February, 1862. Stand with me on the levee. There are from 50 to 100 steamboats lying along the bank, with volumes of black smoke rolling up from their tall chimneys. Among them are gunboats, a cross between a float-ing fort, a dredging machine and a mud-scow. The sailors call them "mud-turkles."

"There are thousands of soldiers on the steamboats and on the shore, waiting for the sailing of the expedition which is to make an opening in the line of Rebel defenses; thousands of people busy as bees loading and unloading steamboats, rolling barrels and boxes. Thousands of men and thousands of mules and horses.

"It is Sunday. A sweet day of rest in peaceful times, but in war there is not much observance of the Sabbath. It is midwinter, but a south-wind sweeps up the Mississippi, so mild and balmy that the bluebirds and robins are out. Steamboats are crowded with troops, waiting for orders to sail, they know not where.

"The shops are open, the soldiers are purchasing knickknacks, tobacco, pipes, paper and pens to send letters to loved ones far away. At a gingerbread stall, a half-dozen are taking lunch. The oyster saloons are crowded. Boys are crying their newspapers. There are laughable and solemn scenes. Yonder is a hospital. A file of soldiers stand waiting in the street. A coffin is brought out. The fife begins its mournful air, the drum its muffled beat. The procession moves away, bearing the dead soldier to his silent home. A few months ago he was a citizen, cultivating his farm upon the prairies, ploughing, sowing, reaping. But now the great reaper, Death.

"The church-bells toll the hour. Some remember that it is Sunday and wade through the muddy streets to the church. Half the congregation are from the Army and Navy. Commodore Foote is there, a devout worshiper. Before church he visited each gunboat of this fleet.

"Let us on Monday accept the kind invitation of Commodore Foote and go on board his flagship and make an inspection of this strange-looking craft. It is like a great box on a raft. The sides are inclined, made of stout oak timbers and plated with iron. You enter through a porthole, where you may lay your hand upon the iron lips of a great gun, which throws a ball nine inches in diameter. There are 14 guns, with stout oaken carriages.

"Commodore Foote points out to you a secluded corner, where any one of the crew who loves to read his Bible and hold secret devotions may do so and not be disturbed. He has given a library of good books to the crew, and he has persuaded them that it will be better for them to give up their allowance of grog than to drink it. He walks among the men, and has a kind word for all. Will they not fight bravely under such a commander?

"On Monday afternoon, February 2nd, the gunboats Cincinnati, Essex, St. Louis, Carondelet, Lexington, Tyler and Conestoga sailed from Cairo, accompanied by several river steamboats with 10 regiments of troops. They went up the Ohio to Paducah, and entered the Tennessee River at dark. The next morning, about daylight, they anchored a few miles below Fort Henry.

"Looking up the river from the deck of one of Commodore Foote's gunboats, you see Panther Island, which is a mile from the fort. It is a long, narrow sand-bank, covered with a thicket of willows. There is the fort on the eastern bank.

You can count the guns, 17 in all. They are nearly all pivoted, so they may be pointed down the river against the boats, or inland upon the troops. It will not be an easy matter to take the fort from the land side.

"Commodore Foote has planned how to take the fort. General Grant and Commodore Foote agreed that the gunboats should commence the attack at twelve o'clock. The Commodore said, 'I shall commence firing when I reach the head of Panther Island, and it will take me about an hour to reach the fort, for I shall steam up slowly.'

"To his crews, Commodore Foote said, 'Fire slowly, and with deliberate air. If you fire slowly, you will keep cool yourselves, and make every shot count.'

"The gunboats steam up slowly against the current. The boats reach the head of the island, and the fort is in full view. It is thirty-four minutes past twelve o'clock. There is a flash, and a great creamy cloud of smoke. An eight-inch shell screams through the air. Your watch ticks 15 seconds before you hear from it.

"You see a puff of smoke, a cloud of sand thrown up in the fort, and then hear the explosion. From each vessel a shell is thrown. The fort accepts the challenge, and instantly the 12 guns which are in position to sweep the river, open upon the advancing boats. The shot and shell plough furrows in the stream, and throw columns of water high in the air. The gunboats move straight on."

Dear Readers of the *My Folks* series, is it not a rare privilege to savor these words from the lips, as it were, of one who can recount so vividly what it was like for those folks who fought the Civil War?

From *My Days And Nights On the Battle-Field* by Charles Coffin.

Marcia Baker Pogue
Cincinnati, Ohio

From A History Of The Army Life Of Matt Jennings

"After night I was placed by Lt. C. C. World on picket between the two lines in darkness by myself. I lay in some leaves in a kind of a sink and it was cold and I could hear my teeth chatter and being but a few steps from the enemy, I feared they could hear and I would be captured.

"Next morning the battle was renewed with vigor, lasting during the morning as the enemy began a hasty retreat. Our boys pursued them hastily with yells and firing until we reached the main battleground where a mansion the day before was struck with our shells and set on fire and burned. Their dead men lay with their clothes burned off of them and they lay so thick on the ground, we could scarcely find places for our feet.

"We could yell no more."

Ruth (Jennings) Wilson
Peculiar, Missouri

MY FOLKS AND THE CIVIL WAR

CHAPTER 4: Survival On The Front Lines

Finer Than Peace Time Bread

My grandfather was a member of an Indiana Volunteer company that served thru the Civil War with the Union Army. He has often told of the food scarcity for the soldiers during the last campaigns.

The Southerners burned all supplies they could not carry as they retreated. The farmers had so little for the Quartermasters to confiscate, and supply lines were too long to provide for all their needs.

The soldiers were often so hungry that they would go to the feeding places of the mules and salvage the corn knocked from their feed boxes. They washed the corn and parched it on shovels held over the fires. Grandfather said it tasted better to him than the finest bread eaten in peace time.

Clarice Rhoads
Green Castle, Missouri

Mumps Add To War Woes

Among the treasured keepsakes handed down to our generation of the family from our great-grandfather, who was a Captain in the Civil War, are his blue cap, his discharge certificate, a portion of his diary and the watch he carried through the War.

The Captain was still a Corporal when the following excerpts were written in his neat, legible handwriting. All were written in 1863.

"We were busy all day pitching camp. Cold rain night and day. I now go to the Surgeon with the sick."

"Rain and cold again today. Three of our men had half their heads shaved for being drunk. Could get no news from Hooker's Army."

"Bright and warm. At 15 minutes to 2 p.m., we had news of the capture of Richmond by General Dix. Hope it is so. After dress parade we received news that the Star-Spangled Banner waves over Richmond. The news was received with cheers and patriotic speeches until a late hour. God grant this War may soon close and I can come home to enjoy the blessings of peace!"

"A stormy day. In the evening we were paid two months' pay. Received $36.30."

"Saw General Grant today. At 12:00 at night, heavy firing was heard in the direction of Vicksburg. Over 60 reports of cannon in a minute."

"The Rebs asked to have the firing stopped until four o'clock so they could bury their dead. Then we laid in the woods all day, the next day firing at the Rebs and they at us."

"Our company went on picket but I was so sick I stayed in camp."

"We marched at noon but I had to be carried in the ambulance wagon. Got a pass from Surgeon Prince for myself and 11 men to ride."

"I suffered very much from fever. Men have died from heat. Before night we crossed the Big Black, and the ambulance carried us to the hospital where we all took quinine."

"Another day in the hospital with the shakes. Passed a hard day. Large bumps behind each ear."

"Doctor says I have the mumps. My face continues to swell and aches very bad."

"My health is improving. Our Doctor's name is Norton, a Massachusetts man. Captain Draper came to see me. I have had a long time suffering with my neck."

Mary Hall
Beverly, Kansas

Honey For The Hardtack

Grandfather served four full years in the 9th Illinois Cavalry with the troops in the West, as he called it, meaning along the Mississippi River and the Southwestern states.

Somewhere in the campaigns the men were running short of supplies and were tired of the hardtack they were issued. Grandfather spied some beehives near a farmhouse and thought how good honey would taste. Under cover of darkness, he grabbed a hive and away he ran. He was fleet of foot and was making good progress back to his companions when he tripped and fell.

Out came the bees, humming angrily. Grandfather was determined not to lose the honey, so he picked himself up and ran on, stinging bees and all. The boys had their honey and Grandfather had numerous bee stings.

Sometime after this, the cavalry had to dismount and advance on foot. Grandfather was delegated to remain in the rear to hold the reins of his comrade's horses. While doing this, a stray shot struck him in the knee, disabling him for some time. After recovering, he rejoined his company, serving until the end of the War. He was with the troops who marched down Pennsylvania Avenue to be reviewed by President Lincoln.

He often spoke of Mother Bickerdyke, the brave woman who did so much by her nursing to relieve the suffering of sick and injured men. He said she was like an angel to the troops.

As long as Grandfather lived, he retained the erect military bearing he acquired during the four years of the Civil War.

Gladys Meyer
Omaha, Nebraska

"Sow Bosom" And Beans

My father was a Union Civil War veteran. He was a blacksmith and working at the job in Centerville, Iowa, when they were asking for volunteers. He took off his leather apron and went out and joined Company I, 3rd Iowa Cavalry. He was a young man with a wife and little daughter nine months old. That was quite a long time before I was born.

He told the story that at one time during the service they had been on "sow bosom" and beans till they were really hungry for a change. He and some more of the boys found a calf and they butchered it. Of course, that was against the rules and somebody told the commanding officer. He in turn called my father on the carpet.

Father said he combed his hair and shined up his shoes and went as he was told, but he took some of that nice fresh meat and gave it to the officer.

That did the trick, he didn't get reprimanded as he expected.

M. C. Mendenhall
Weldona, Colorado

A Pipe And Gunpowder

Our favorite story goes back to the Civil War. It concerns our great-grandfather who was a raw recruit, an overgrown Indiana farm boy at 16.

After joining up, he was assigned as a teamster in the Indiana Regulars of the Union forces. One of his first jobs was to take his team of mules and an open wagon to haul a load of loose gunpowder to the front lines.

At this time, Grandad, like so many soldiers, smoked a pipe whenever he had the opportunity. This time was no different. After he loaded his wagon, he lit his pipe and started to return to the armory. One of the first things to happen was that the wagon hit a bump and caused a spark to fly out of his pipe and ignite the gunpowder.

His report stated that nearly one-half bushel of the gunpowder burned before he could get the fire stamped out. They didn't even charge him with destroying government property!

Rex O. Wonnell
San Jose, California

Turkey And Dressing

My grandfather, born in Virginia, came to Missouri when he was a boy in his teens.

When the Civil War broke out he was so anxious to enlist that he lied about his age and was accepted in the Southern Army.

He served under General Lee, and more than once he saw Lee give his shoes to a soldier with sore and bleeding feet.

The Southern soldiers were always hungry, especially for meat. Once Grandpa spied a turkey gobbler alongside the road as they marched along. He gave his gun to the soldier behind him and made him promise to answer roll call for him.

Then he threw his blanket over the turkey and carried him into camp, dressed and cooked him at night over an open fire outside. He visited a farmhouse and asked the farmer's wife for some cold biscuits to make dressing. She gave him some, and later he returned to bring her some turkey and dressing. She told him it was delicious.

When the War was over, Grandpa did not wait to be mustered out, but set out for home immediately, wearing a new uniform and carrying his gun. He was captured by a man who stole his gun and uniform and released him.

Mrs. Earl James
Paris, Missouri

Meat For The Officers

Another incident told by my grandfather: A soldier went out at night, got him some meat and would dress it and hang it up by his tent. In the morning it would be gone. When he went down by the officers' tent, they would always have meat to eat.

One night he killed a dog, dressed it nice and put it in the same place. Sure enough next morning it was gone also. So again he visited the officers' tent. Sure enough they had meat, and he began to laugh until the officers demanded why he was laughing.

He said, "Oh! I was just wondering how that dog meat tasted."

He dressed other meat out later, but it was always there next morning. As we know, the Civil War Vets had to rustle some of their eats, they weren't given eats as our boys are today.

Cora Stout
Clifton, Colorado

Rattlesnake Repast

My grandfather was a Civil War veteran. He was in Company A of the First Iowa Cavalry. He was sent to Burlington, Iowa, then on to the battlefields at Sedalia, Missouri.

His first Captain was Dinsmore.

At Fort Smith he was so ill he was taken to a hospital where he remained for four months. Then he returned to his cavalry at Chalk Bluffs. Here the country was full of big rattlesnakes and one night when the men were all lying in line of battle, Grandfather was at one end of the line. He was thinking of the rattlesnakes, when he felt one crawl over him. He lay real still and it crawled clear on down the line of soldiers. Next morning they followed its trail in the dust and found it in a thicket. It had fourteen rattles and had swallowed two squirrels.

The soldiers thought it would be great sport to be able to say they had eaten rattlesnake. Grandfather was a cook in the Army, so he very carefully dressed and cooked the huge snake and they ate it. Many times they had very little to eat.

Fern Boyles
Woodburn, Iowa

Starvation Rations

During the Civil War my great-grandfather and others of his troop were in an old fort surrounded by the enemy. They ran out of food and before long were desperate. They kept thinking help would come to rescue them.

The old fort was badly infested with rats. As starving men have no choice, they killed rats, skinned them and cooked them in a big iron kettle.

Grandfather has been dead many years, but I remember sitting on his lap to hear the story and him saying, "I do declare, that was good soup, but we were hungry enough to eat anything!"

P. S. They were rescued before the rats played out.

Norma Johnson
Sentinel, Oklahoma

Captain On The Spot

My father was born in Ohio in 1837. He enlisted in the Union Army and served under John T. Sherman and was in the famous March to the Sea. He told some amusing stories, and this one I remember.

They were in camp but had not been in combat for several days. A nice fat pig came by the cook's tent and the boys planned to get that pig. They got it, skinned it, and burned or buried the skin to avoid being caught. They cooked part of the meat but had quite a piece left.

The next day a woman came down hunting her pig. Said she was sure the boys had killed it. The Captain, who had a private tent the boys seldom entered, said, "Oh, I'm sure you are mistaken. I haven't a boy in my company that would do such a thing. I'll order all tents searched."

Meanwhile the boys had slipped around while he was talking and put the meat in the back of the Captain's tent. All tents were searched but no meat found. Then the Captain, always a gentlemen, said, "Search my tent now."

And there they found the meat. The embarrassed Captain found it hard to explain.

Lida Price
Fair Play, Missouri

Feathers And All

My grandfather was a Civil War veteran, having enlisted (not drafted) in the 100th Illinois Regiment. He used to tell us of being so exhausted and hungry one day. They had no food supply trucks, camp kitchens or even cooks. They had to "forage" for their eats. He got a chicken, and as time was short before they had to move on, there was no time to properly dress it. They threw it into a pot and boiled it, feathers and all!

After that, my granddaddy could never bear the thought of stewed chicken.

Mrs. Albert Lundeen
Skidmore, Missouri

Wash Before Eating

My father-in-law told of how happy they were when folks living near their camp came with donations of food, especially home-cooked. One lady brought a particularly appetizing huge dish of some meaty substance. All ate of it with gusto, until one fellow remarked that was the best blood pudding he had ever tasted. Most of the partakers immediately lost their appetites.

Boys used to bring huge pailfuls of delicious black-berries, which they sold for a mere pittance. All wondered how they managed to get so many so quickly, until they happened to come onto them in the woods shaking the heavily laden bushes into a filthy washtub. After that, they washed the fruit before eating.

Mrs. Bert Stewart
Springville, Iowa

Camp Prices

Two letters written in 1863 by my husband's uncle during the War are treasured keepsakes. One is written at Camp Natchez, Mississippi, September 28, 1863; and the other at General Hospital, Ward No. 2, Vicksburg, Mississippi, on December 29, 1863.

He became ill and died at the age of 20 a few months before the end of the War. So many soldiers became ill because they did not have the food a sick person should have. Quoting from one of his letters:

"Potatoes are worth $4.00 a bushel, green apples 5 cents apiece, eggs are worth 90 cents a dozen, chickens a dollar apiece, milk 29 cents a quart, butter 90 cents a pound, and canned fruit still dearer, yet I might go on and mention a dozen different articles that sell at the same rate. Everything is dear here."

Lois Decker
Concordia, Kansas

Shirt Story

Among the war stories Grandpa would tell was one about a certain young man in his Regiment who was always stealing any little thing he could from the boys. So one time when he stole a shirt, the officers thought they would break him of it by making him go around to every tent in the camp, putting his head inside and saying, "I stole a shirt." It worked — the embarrassment of it all broke him of that for good.

Mrs. M. O. Paxton
Lenexa, Kansas

General Result

When the Army would be camping near my grand-father's farm, my grandmother would send my father and uncle with baskets of homemade pies to sell to the soldiers. If anyone along the way had pies or a message, they would take that, also. One morning they started early for the camp with two baskets of pies. A mile from their home lived a widow who was famous for serving dinners to the Generals of the Armies passing thru. She asked the boys where they were going, and who was the General?

The boys said there had been a battle, but they had not heard the General result. She clapped her hands with glee and said, "I have never fed General Result, so you Boys be sure to bring him here to dinner."

Mrs. John A. Kuntz
Denver, Colorado

CHAPTER 5: Hardtack And Cornmeal

Shingles For Soles And Corn To Eat

My own grandfather, Elisha Miller, fought in the Civil War. He was a small man, five foot and one inch tall. He was visiting in our home when I was in seventh or eighth grade and I went to school and told what he had related to me. It was the only time I ever got a good grade in history. History was not my favorite subject.

He spent many nights sleeping on the ground without food, and he crawled beneath the horses' heads and picked up whole grain corn (horses cannot eat without dropping some out of their mouths). He ate the corn and was glad to get it. Had he been caught by his superiors, he could have been shot. He lived to be 91 years old.

He also told about the soles wearing out on his shoes (everyone else's also). He found cardboard or roofing shingles and put them inside his shoes. When they came to rivers, they waded across and if the water was deep, other soldiers carried him either on their backs or a "pack saddle, " made by two men.

Verna L. Jestes
LaMar, Missouri

Welcome Water — Even From Pasture Piles

My maternal Connecticut grandfather served with the "boys in blue" and was a cavalry man. I remember him well with his long white beard, but because I was a small child when I knew him, I didn't appreciate or value the few things he told. He was always reticent about his War experiences, and that chapter of his life had to be passed from Mother to me.

On reconnaissance one day in Virginia the riders came upon a lovely Southern mansion where a slave was holding his master's saddled horse. Grandfather, whose horse had been shot from under him, and being fleet of foot, kept up with his detachment for three days, saw his chance to get another mount. He drew his revolver and creeping through the shrubbery, accosted the slave. "Give me the horse or I'll shoot you dead," he said quietly. A few days later Grandfather declared he saw that same man in Northern territory, free from his master's wrath.

Another time significant in his memory was that while on a flanking maneuver, provisions became exhausted, and they knew extreme hunger. Seeing a cow in a pasture, they slaughtered it, tore the meat apart and ate like ravenous wolves. They had no water to drink for many, many hours and were almost desperate from heat and thirst. Not long after, they came upon a vacant pasture freshly wet from heavy rain, with water filling the dried dung. The men dismounted, and lying flat on their stomachs, drank their fill of the newly-fallen rain. "Never had water tasted so good to man or beast," Grandfather admitted.

Mrs. L. J. Tomlinson
Onslow, Iowa

U.S. Means US

When quite young, I often listened to my father tell stories of the Civil War, some too depressive to mention and others of laughter, daring and love. I mention the one of the camp cook that put in too much rice to cook and it swelled out of bounds, and the foraging raid when one took the crock of butter and broke the crock when scrambling over a stone wall. Also of the quaint character that served as camp aide and was much in demand to bring the boys their coffee when they hollered, "Eli, bring out the coffee," to which he sometimes replied with his vocabulary of cuss words. However, when a fierce battle was on, he risked his life to take the coffee out. Though warned, he replied, "My boys have got to have their coffee."

I have in my possession a packet of letters my father wrote while serving in the Civil War. From one date, May 27, 1863, I quote the following story.

"I have been in a battle. I will give you a brief sketch of a raid we had later in Virginia yesterday. It is against the orders of the Colonel to cross the river. Yesterday morning I and two other soldiers went to the Lieut. to get permission to cross the river. He said he would not give us permission to cross the river. He said he would give us a pass to go and swim; so we went down to the river and made a raft and put our clothes on it and commenced swimming. We kept on swimming till we landed on the other side of the river.

"Our clothes had got wet. We got what water we could out of them and put them on. The other two boys appointed me Capt. and we started off on our mission. We went about one mile from the river and stopped and took dinner with a Rebel. After dinner we hitchhiked about three miles farther, when I got sick of footing it. So I told the boys that if I was commander, we would have some horses.

"We went to a farmer who had three horses. He was just going to work with them. I told him I would like to hire his horses and at the same time took the best one by the bit, threw the harness off, put on a blanket and got on the horse. The other boys did the same.

"We started off toward Leesburg. We went within 2 1/2 miles of Leesburg. We learnt there that there was Rebel cavalry and that they were scouting around everyday. I got a saddle. We then took another road and went about 10 miles toward Harper's Ferry, stirring up the Rebs at every house.

"We then stayed off public roads and kept in the fields and woods till we got back to the Potomac.

"My horse would jump all the fences and ditches. When we got to the place where we were to cross the river, I found my horse was a Government horse. U.S. was marked on his shoulder. I told the boys U.S. meant us. So we took him across and presented him to the Captain."

Mabel Morrison
Monett, Missouri

Chickens For New Year's Dinner

I am 86 years old, the daughter of a Civil War veteran who enlisted August 11, 1862, at 16 years of age, and served until the War's end. I have his cartridge box, belt with large U.S. buckles, his bayonet, cap box, some caps and primers and three bullets which bear marks of use.

I also have two diaries dated 1862 to 1865, which have interesting anecdotes of military life, the hardships and privations suffered, and hope and cheer at doing his duty for his country. Here is one story from his diary.

"Dec. 31, 1862. Jacob Sell, James Palmer and myself went out on a foraging expedition about 2 1/2 miles north of Trenton, then one mile east to the home of an "old Sesesh." He met us at the gate and we asked him politely if he would give us a chicken for New Year's dinner.

He told us he had none. We might have credited his story had not, at that moment, three or four big roosters stepped out from under the house.

Jim hauled away at one and I at another. Jim killed his, but mine I only crippled. I reloaded and shot him. We got one apiece and started off, telling the old man we were "much obliged" to him for them.

He said he wouldn't say we were welcome, so we threw down our chickens and went back and shot four more, which were all we wanted to carry. We left the old man in a violent rage."

Pauline King
Melvern, Kansas

Horse And Rider Drafted

My grandmother had four brothers in the Civil War. My great-grandfather and his sons thought the differences between the North and South should be settled by mediation rather than war.

When George became 18 years of age, he and his horse were drafted into the Confederate Army. It wasn't long before he took measles and some other sickness, so they left him in a tent in some people's yard and told them to take care of him. They didn't take very good care of him, and he almost died. It rained a lot during that time. When he was able, he got on his horse and started home. He had to cross creeks and rivers. When he got to one stream, the water was so swift, he and the horse were swept downstream. George caught onto a tree. A family living nearby came to his rescue. He stayed with them several days. When he recovered from his illness, his outfit was long gone.

Mrs. Gillie Riley
Rogers, Arkansas

Strychnine-Laced Buttermilk

My grandfather was born in 1835, served with Company A, 40th Regiment E.M.M., at Sedalia, Missouri. He suffered many hardships during the Civil War.

My uncle died and Grandfather was called home for the funeral. The night before the funeral, they had gone to bed when they heard the enemy coming. Grandfather escaped thru a back window while Grandmother was opening the front door. Being a beautiful moonlight night, he couldn't go to the barn for his horse without being caught. He was forced to spend a very uncomfortable night in a huge yellow thorny rose bush.

Both sides would go to homes and demand food to be cooked for them. One time the company stopped at a house, where Grandfather knew the woman, but her husband was on the other side and she hated the Union Army soldiers.

She was churning fresh butter when they arrived. Grandfather asked for buttermilk with his meal. He drank it and then screamed, "I am poisoned; don't drink any buttermilk!" The Captain placed his gun to the woman's head and said he would blow out her brains if she didn't tell him what she had put in the buttermilk

She was terrible frightened and after she said strychnine, the Captain went to her herb garden and got calamus, beat it up and gave it to Grandfather and saved his life. My grandmother and my mother always raised calamus.

Mrs. J. F. McKeehan
LaMonte, Missouri

Feasting On Tomatoes

Grandma's husband said he did not like tomatoes till during the War. There was a number of men marching, and they did not have much to eat when they came by the old house where there was a world of ripe tomatoes. The men went to picking them and eating them. Grandpa said he never in his life ate anything that tasted so good. From that day on he liked tomatoes any way they were fixed.

Mrs. Glenn Locke
Alliance, Nebraska

"Can She Bake A Cherry Pie, Billy Boy?"

When the Civil War broke out, my uncle, together with some other boys and young men of his town, answered the call of "Father Abraham." But he was underage and his mother pulled him out, so he had to wait several years to join.

The rations were hardtack, which was almost too hard to eat, and a piece of salt pork, which each had to cook himself. And tho I'm not sure, there may have been coffee and beans, too.

Some of the men improved the ration by raiding the surrounding countryside at night for fresh meat. My uncle accompanied one of these men one night. He got a bad scare when he almost got caught, and he didn't try it again.

In his older years he could still remember and sing songs of Civil War days, like "Marching Thru Georgia" and "Can She Make a Cherry Pie, Billy Boy?".

Paul Tulien
Topeka, Kansas

Kitchen Knife Surgery

My grandfather was fighting in the Confederate Army when he was 16 years old. He was wounded in the shoulder, and my great-grandmother took the bullet out with a kitchen knife. She hid him in a cave near by and slipped out food to him in the dead of the night. When he came out, his hair was snow white.

Clara Comstock
Sparks, Oklahoma

Lamb In Dog's Clothing

My father-in-law was a Civil War soldier when he told me about having measles and sleeping on a brush pile in a clearing with about eight inches of snow on the ground. I thought, "Poor fellow, how did he live over all that?" I heard him tell a neighbor, who was also a veteran, about his regiment passing through a little village in the deep South.

There was a small church and some people were gathered for a funeral. They rode out by the cemetery and took a look around, rode on and made camp about four miles from the cemetery. Under cover of darkness 20 or more men and boys went back and opened the grave. They found a wooden box about four feet wide and deep and eight feet long filled with country cured hams. They took them all back to camp.

Dolly Sanders
Doniphan, Missouri

Frozen To The Pews

I remember many things our Father told us about the Civil War days. He fought with a band of Union soldiers who were fighting a band of guerrillas.

They had been out in the rain, and when night came, they found a country church to sleep in. When morning came, their clothes were frozen to the seats.

Clara Jackson
Corning, Iowa

Bullet-Proof Carpet Roll

I recall the things my father had to tell me about the Civil War. How he marched across the States so much, and while passing a Southern home, he picked up a piece of carpet and said to his comrade, "You will have to carry this, we will need it for a bed."

He folded it and tied it over his comrade's left shoulder and under his right arm, and before night, the Rebels were firing at them. A bullet struck John, his comrade, right over his heart. It knocked him down, but just went through the carpet, so the carpet saved his life.

Nellie Hill
Parsons, Kansas

CHAPTER 6: Bushwhackers and Jayhawkers

Money Safe In Children's Playhouse

When my great-grandmother heard that "bushwhackers" and renegades were in the neighborhood, she took her own money and that of her two daughters, who lived nearby, and hid it in an old broken iron teakettle and set it in the children's playhouse.

Sure enough, a band of thieves came that night and demanded money. When they found none, after tearing up the whole place, they went across the field to my great uncle's home and were so incensed at finding no money, they stole their meat and even the older son's boots.

They upset the barrel of soft soap, turned over the barrel of molasses and even poured kerosene in the barrel of salt and did much other damage.

Lillie B. Reid
Mountain Grove, Missouri

Hard Times Indeed

My mother-in-law's father told this Civil War story about a neighbor family.

Before the father went to war, the mother and father discussed where they would hide their savings during the War, putting it away for hard times. Their "little picker" type daughter overheard them, and knew where the money was hidden.

One day her mother was working in the fields and the little girl was at the house when some guerrilla fighters rode in. After inquiring about her parents, they asked if she had money or anything that could help them. She said they had some money, but they were saving it for "hard times."

"Why, that's who we are!" exclaimed one of the men. "We're Hard Times!

So the little girl got the money and gave it to them.

Mrs. Kenneth Heistand
Columbus, Kansas

Hold-Up At Mt. Zion Church

During the Civil War, when my grandfather, William Butler Barlow, was a boy of 14, he was attending morning services at Mt. Zion Methodist Church in Washington County, Kentucky, when it was surrounded by guerrillas.

He said that the first hints he had that something was wrong was when the church all at once began to grow dark, and he saw several men drop their pocketbooks into their boot tops. Looking toward the windows, he saw a man sitting on a horse at each window with a drawn gun, while others entered the church and robbed the members of their money and any other valuable belongings.

Then, before leaving, the guerrillas exchanged their worn horses for the better ones belonging to the congregation and rode away.

Frances Anderson
Louisville, Kentucky

Valuable Hair-Do

How Grandmother hid money from the bushwhackers is our favorite Civil War story. She was the second wife of Grandfather and much younger. He did not fight in the War, but had several brothers fighting for the South.

He had turned against slavery when he was a boy on his father's plantation in Virginia. Grandmother's brothers were fighting for the North.

Soldiers of both families sent what money they could to her for safekeeping. She had long thick hair which she wore in rolls, hair around currency. Bushwhackers turned the place upside down, including the smokehouse floor and the ash hopper, but Grandma held her head high as she sat on the porch churning.

Sorry to say, some she saved was worthless.

Mrs. Paul Morrow
Boonville, Missouri

Big Red Ants Three Times A Day

My grandfather and my father and four other brothers fought in the Civil War. I remember Father telling this story.

As the Army was passing a house they heard a woman scream. Father and two others stopped to see what was the reason for the screams, and they stayed long enough for Father to help deliver a baby. He was only 19 years old, the youngest of the three. The other two said "no," and they got so far behind the Army that a bunch of bushwhackers run them off into the Mississippi River bottom.

Kept them hiding for four days without food. They chopped in the rotten logs and scooped up big red ants by the handful and ate them. The ants were so stiff and cold that they never stung their tongues, and he said it would surprise you how good they tasted.

Sarah Davidson
Neosho, Missouri

Burned Out By Bushwhackers

My favorite story took place a few months before my grand-dad was born, but he'd heard it told so many times and could tell it with so much feeling, it seemed he was there when it happened.

His father had gone off to war, as had all able-bodied, brave and honest men, he'd always tell us. His two-year-old son and his wife, who was expecting another child (my grandfather), were left alone in their small cabin in Cedar County, Missouri, several miles from any neighbor.

She did her best to make a living with her garden plot and milk cows. She wouldn't have thought of leaving her home and going back to live with her parents. She was only one of many who were left behind to keep the home fires burning. The men didn't plan to be gone but a short time.

I wish I had the space and ability to put on paper the horror and agony I felt as Grandfather came to the part when the bushwhackers came and took all the food in the house and told her and her son to get out. Then they burned her house before her eyes with her pleading for mercy.

Mrs. L. G. Minson
Afton, Oklahoma

Grandma Puts Curse On Raiders

This is one of the Civil War stories my grandma told me. As did most families in those days, the men went to war, and the women did the best they could. My grandma was alone with the children, my mother 10 years and her brother six. There were men who did not join the Army, called bushwhackers, who formed gangs and took what they wanted.

They came to Grandma's home and found her meat salted down in the corner of her home, and they said she had probably poisoned it, so decided to do something mean.

They ripped her featherbed, poured it in the floor, then poured a large crock of honey into the feathers. Not satisfied with this, they tore her wall clock down with a bayonet. One rode away on her riding mare she had hidden in the smokehouse, and as Grandma held onto the bridle, this man, whom she had known a long while, kicked her down. Grandma was superstitious and believed she put a curse on him, that he should not live to ride her mare. He had always been cruel, and his own followers feared him. As he rode through a creek bed, he was shot. No one knew who did it.

After many weary months my grandma and family went north to Springfield, Illinois, to make their home.

Ida Bellinger
Kansas City, Kansas

Grandfather Hides In Cave

One of my grandfathers was a Confederate soldier and was captured and taken to prison. In a few months, he was offered his freedom if he would swear allegiance to the Constitution and promise never to take up arms against the Government again. This he gladly did, but because of the guerrilla warfare or "bushwhackers," he was never able to go home but lived in caves nearby until the end of the War. Grandmother would take corn bread and fried pork in a sack and put it up in a tree every few days for him to get when he came out. Once a big snow kept him in for several days. Grandmother managed to raise enough corn for cornmeal and the hogs were fattened on mast (acorns).

Once the bushwhackers took the featherbed from the children's bed, cut the corner and scattered feathers for miles down the road.

Mrs. John Reagan
Waverly, Kansas

Bushwhackers Worse Than Soldiers

Grandmother lived in Missouri between the North and South. Soldiers from both Armies would come by and eat everything they could find in the house. They would kill and eat a cow or calf, and what they couldn't eat, they took with them.

The bushwhackers were worse than the soldiers. They had killed all the livestock and chickens except one old hen that managed to escape. My aunts and Grandmother decided to have her for Sunday dinner before the bushwhackers could get her.

The dinner was nearly ready when they saw the bushwhackers coming down the road. They grabbed the old hen and buried her in the garden. They searched the house but the dinner was safe.

My uncle was in the Northern Army, and when they were camped close to home he would come home. They were camped near Chillhowee, and one dark cloudy night he walked home. Some of our close neighbors were bushwhackers and were waiting for him. Grandmother had a one and a half story house and part of the family would keep watch from the upstairs window. During the night they saw the bushwhackers coming, and my uncle climbed out one of the upstairs windows onto the roof. He hid behind a large fireplace chimney. They watched the house for a long time before they finally gave up. He got back to camp safely.

Mrs. Sally Boone
Clinton, Missouri

Warning Saves Neighbors

This is a happening in Civil War days in Jefferson County, Missouri. I have often heard my father tell this story to my grandfather. It was perilous times in those days. One night a bunch of bushwhackers came to my grandfather's home about 1 a.m. at night. There was about 18 inches of snow on the ground and they called him out in his nightclothes and no shoes.

They made him walk over a mile to show them the road to a neighbor's house so they could rob it. The man had several hundred dollars. Somehow my grandfather got word to him the bushwhackers were going to rob him that night.

Grandfather told the man to take his family and to not let any one know where they were at. And they did. Grandfather saved his money and his home. They did not burn his home, but went to another and robbed it. Grandfather finally returned home, almost frozen in his bare feet and no clothes but his night clothes. Father and Grandmother sat up and listened while he was expecting any minute to hear the gunfire killing his father. No one ever knew where my grandfather ever got the information that the robbers were coming.

If they had suspected him he would never have returned home, but he showed them the road, and they let him return home before they went to the other place.

May Davis
Crocker, Missouri

A Happy Ending For One Family

Below you will find a true story of the Civil War days, that happened in this community of Guthrie, Callaway County, Missouri.

I am the granddaughter of a Civil War veteran, Robert W. Emmons. My father, Sterling Price Emmons, was seven months old when things were in a bad condition in this community.

Grandfather had been working all day hiding his and Grandmother's new saddles (one a sidesaddle), bridles, two or three cured hams and all their most prized possessions under the floor of their two room log cabin one mile west of where we (my husband and I) now live. He had taken up some of the oak flooring (which was not tongue and groove) in the corner next to the kitchen and under the bed. There they hid their things, then nailed down the flooring again. The other side of the Army would take whatever they wanted if it could be found.

Grandfather was called for duty the same evening only a few miles away. He grabbed his musket, put some biscuits and fried ham in his pocket, kissed his wife and sick baby and went out into the cold, snowy, late November night.

My father was sick with a cold, croup and ear trouble and cried all night long.

About 10 p.m. the same evening, some of the other side came and took all the food they could find and two of Grandfather's best riding horses from a pasture nearby. (Grandmother was a great horsewoman so Grandfather kept good riding horses.) They found the old saddles and bridles at the barn, so on they went, not knowing about the new ones.

About midnight a young man of the community knocked on the door and called Grandmother by name, saying, "Nancy, Bob has been shot. I think he is dead by now, and some of us will get the body home when daylight comes."

Grandmother lived a thousand years during the next five hours with her husband dead and her only child very sick. By now she thought he had double pneumonia. She had no food in the house, just hams under a nailed down floor. Their only heat was from two fireplaces, they cooked on the one in the kitchen. There was no more cut up wood at the woodpile. The coal oil jug was empty and the lamp was getting low after an all night burn with the sick child. No telephone in those days, and by now, the snow was six or eight inches deep and not a neighbor within two or three miles.

About five o'clock the same night someone knocked on the door. She said, "Who's thar?" The knocker said, "It's me, Bob." She said, "The law me, I thought you were dead."

He said, "I was only slightly hit in my left arm, but I thought I was sure to die out in that awful weather and told them to get you word next morning, but they came right on."

What a happy reunion, and my father was soon better.

Many times we grandchildren heard our grandparents tell of this terrible experience of the Civil War days with such a happy ending.

Mrs. Wallace H. Jones
New Bloomfield, Missouri

Women Kept Home Fires Burning

My grandfather was a soldier of the Civil War in the Union Army. But he died long before my grandmother, and I remember most the stories she told of hard times when the women were left alone to take care of the homes and farms while the men were away fighting the War.

My grandmother always said the worst to contend with was the "bushwhackers," and you just better not mention "Rebel Soldiers," or you received a tongue lashing from her.

She told me that when a child died, the women had to dig the grave and make the coffin and bury the child.

She told me of a man coming home to see his family and how he was caught and a sabre ran through his stomach, and how he tightened his belt around him, holding his guts in until he got home, where he died.

She told how the women had to go in a group to the spring for water. And when they went to a salt lick for salt, it became so dangerous for the women because of the bushwhackers catching the women, that they went to the smokehouse and dug up the dirt where the meat had dripped on the ground floor and boiled that and somehow got salt from that.

She told me how the War came close and the houses were shot full of holes, and how one old man had had the women prop him up with pillars, and although he was shot full of holes, he kept shooting back until he was shot through the head and killed. The War, as it was always called, had no glory for my grandmother, to her it was only bitterness and hurt.

Ruby Wilson
Pomona, Missouri

Gathering Around The Teakettle

The one thing I prize most of my antique collection is an iron teakettle my grandparents started housekeeping with in January 1856. Grandmother died when Mother was two years old. Grandfather took her and lived with his mother until the Civil War broke out, then he went into the service. No man could stay home. Old men too feeble for service were killed by the bushwhackers in that part of the country. Women and children were alone and scared to death all the time. Mother said there would come a runner telling them the "Flopp Ear'd Dutch" were coming, killing all women and children.

And as many as the log cabin would accommodate would gather to Grannie's house, put the children to bed. They would make coffee and tea in this teakettle while they watched all night.

Mother said often the "Flopp Ear'd Dutch" never came, and would have been their friends, not foes, had they known it.

Grandfather came through the War okay and lived until February 25, 1912.

Mrs. Chas Newman
Rogersville, Missouri

"Don't Burn My Little Children Up"

My great-grandfather was a soldier in the Missouri Militia. I never saw him as he disappeared or was killed during the War, but I have sat for hours listening to my great-grandmother tell Civil War stories. One outstanding story she told was of the bushwhackers, as she called them.

One night she and her four small children were sitting on the bed, wondering where Great-grandfather was, when the bushwhackers slammed her door open, and asked where Great-grandfather was. Great-grandmother told them she did not know. One of them grabbed up the broom, stuck it into the fire, and with the flaming broom started toward the bed and the little children.

"Oh my God, don't burn my little children up!" She said to her surprise and relief the man stopped, looked at her and left.

I'm the great-granddaughter of a very courageous little Civil War widow.

Eva Garner
Copan, Oklahoma

The Knock At The Door

Having heard many stories of the Civil War from my mother, handed down from her parents, I believe this period must have been as dreadful for those left at home as the men at the front. A

100

knock at the door at night could mean bloodshed and terror. One grandfather was an officer in the Infantry, was captured and in a Southern prison for months, but came home to live out his natural years. The other was home for a brief visit with his family when a knock sounded upon the front door.

Everyone froze where they were. Bushwhackers were on the prowl and no man was safe. Slipping out a side window, Grandfather hid in a hillside cave all through the bitter cold night. He was stricken with pneumonia, a fatal thing in those days, and died within the week, a victim of the Civil War as much as those who were killed in battle.

A neighbor did not escape when the knock came at his home. He was taken to the hillside and shot where he stood.

Fear was everywhere in those days; windows must be cautiously covered, not a glimmer of light shown when darkness came. There was not only fear, there was loneliness, isolation and actual hunger. And it seems the scars of hatred still remain, each blaming the other for the War and its results.

The War was fought by young men, I believe. Even the Generals were young. This was to be a war to end all wars, but it is always so, we hope. Let us keep praying that wars shall cease and difficulties be settled by peaceful means.

Ohla Edwards
Leawood, Kansas

Ambushed At A Creek

During the Civil War, my husband's great-uncle came home one night. The next morning the younger brother put on his soldier brother's coat and cap and took the brother's horse to the creek for water.

Coming back to the house, he saw wild turkey tracks. He thought he would follow them, hoping to get a turkey for dinner.

He saw a purse laying on the ground and when he got off the horse to pick it up, two men began to shoot at him from the bushes.

The cavalry horse was trained, so he stood still and threw his head down.

The boy had no choice but to fight or be killed. He grabbed his brother's gun, killed one man and crippled the other. He followed the bloody tracks of the crippled one to a neighbor house.

Mrs. J. F. McKeehan
La Monte, Missouri

Father Killed Trying To Save Family

My grandfather was killed by what was called then as bushwhackers near Rogers, Arkansas. He being near home had come home for dinner. When he was eating, he saw three men coming.

Realizing his family would be endangered, he got on his horse and could have gotten away, but turned back to shoot at them. They got him, then came on to the house, set it on fire.

Grandma and seven children, with all they could get with one horse, went to Springfield, Missouri, on foot.

Cora Stout
Clifton, Colorado

The Memory And A Gravestone

During the time when border warfare raged in Missouri, a respected young man went out early one morning to cut wood. He rode a handsome horse, and suddenly a band of bushwhackers appeared and demanded the horse.

When he was reluctant to part with it, he was shot. His wife and two small girls were left alone, and one later became my grandmother. Today, there is only the memory and a gravestone in a windswept country churchyard.

Elaine Derendinger
New Franklin, Missouri

Smallpox Ploy Saves Wheat

During the Civil War my father's family lived in Polk County, Missouri. Two of his uncles served in the homeguard, a militia organized by the government to protect the local area from Confederate "bushwhackers.

After being mustered out in 1863, my great-uncle was on his way home with several other Union men when they were captured by some local Confederate sympathizers wearing Union uniforms. They were taken to a schoolhouse in northeast Cedar County and executed. This aroused so much hatred in the area that the captain of the bushwhackers left for the duration of the War.

After the War was over, hearing that the captain was home, my grandfather, who was too young for military service during the War, and was probably only about 16 at the time, saddled up, and with some friends, rode into Cedar County to find him and avenge the killing. At the man's farmhouse, his wife told them he wasn't at home. Then they saw him running from the back of the house to a horse he had waiting for a quick escape.

They all fired, but only one hit him, they didn't know which, but he was down with an ugly wound on his neck, and they left, thinking he was dead. They probably didn't stay around long to see, for it was against the law to kill Confederates after the War was over. But there wasn't much organized law at that time. He didn't die, his wife nursed him back to health, and years later, he could be seen in public with a big scar on his neck.

My grandmother Carter was born in northwest Arkansas, when she was about 12, she heard the guns of the Battle of Pea Ridge. During that time the area was full of soldiers looking for food, or anything else they could steal. Her family had lost all their livestock, and the men had all left home. There was only she, her mother and the other children, and all they had for food was a large bin of crushed wheat that was kept hidden under a bed.

One day one of the girls came down with a minor fever and she was put in the bed. Then some soldiers came looking for food, and as one of them approached the bed, he noticed the sick girl. "What's wrong with that girl?" he asked.

Their mother told him, "I'm afraid she's got the smallpox, there's a lot of it around." Hearing that, the soldiers left in a hurry, thus saving their precious bin of wheat.

V. E. Carter
Topeka, Kansas

The Great Salt Trip

It is well known that, during the Civil War, the North had greater supplies of guns, gunpowder, railroads, steel, uniforms, shoes and food than the South. Less known is the fact that the Confederacy was in dire need of a precious commodity, salt. The shortage was felt as early as 1861 when the South lost the salt works at Charleston, Virginia. It produced 7,000 bushels of salt per day, enough to supply the entire Confederacy. In New Orleans, salt was worth $1 per sack while cotton was $160 a bale. On November 18, salt brought $1.10 a lb. at auction. The next day it brought $1.30 a lb.

As the War drug on, in the small towns of the South, salt might not be available at any price. That was the case in Evening Shade, Arkansas, where people boiled the soil from smokehouse floors to regain the salt that had fallen to the earth in past years. The situation was so critical that in one of the late War years, a group of local citizens organized an expedition to the Missouri bootheel to obtain a supply of salt. One member of that expedition, Charles Shaver, wrote in the *Sharp County Record* in 1901, details of what came to be known as "the salt trip."

Three wagons pulled by oxen left Evening Shade in early October of one year late in the War. The wagons were loaded with bales of cotton, which they hoped to sell in Missouri in order to buy much-needed supplies, particularly salt.

Everything went well until they reached a point near Crowley's Ridge. There they encountered a band of jayhawkers who demanded tribute. Jayhawkers were ruffians who professed Union allegiance but were more intent on gaining booty. Southern bands of this ilk were called bushwhackers. Two jayhawkers rolled a bale of cotton off Charles Shaver's wagon before allowing the wagons to continue. The 450-lb. bale would have brought over $400 in New Madrid, so it was no small loss.

The Arkansans took their cotton into New Madrid where it brought 95 cents a pound. Charles Shaver even used the cotton from his mattress to piece out a bale. After making some purchases, they returned to their camp near Point Pleasant. It was dark when they arrived. The men were feeding the oxen, and the women were cooking the evening meal when a band of blue-clad jayhawkers burst into the camp firing their guns. They ordered the travelers to surrender their valuables at once.

The travelers felt great relief to find themselves back on the soil of Arkansas. But, the first four miles were covered by more than a foot of water with no visible road to follow. They had to move slowly through the timber until they reached higher ground. At Crowley's Ridge, an old clock peddler invited them to spend the night in one room of his house. The peddler's wife let the women raid her cabbage patch, and the weary travelers enjoyed a sumptuous meal of cabbage and pork.

The trip from the Cache River was in familiar surroundings and proved uneventful. Charles Shaver wrote, "When I got home, I had been gone five weeks and four days. I had slept on a bed two nights and in a house only six or seven times. Along with the others, I was exposed to the elements of rain, snow, sleet and cold. I weighed 95 pounds when I returned."

Sam Thompson
Evening Shade, Arkansas

CHAPTER 7: Prisons – Misery And Miracles

Angel In Snow-White Garments

My great-grandfather Thomas was a Civil War veteran that fought thru many of the hardest battles of the Civil War. Battle of Antietam, of Chicamaugua, Bull Run, as well as the other hard battles fought during the Civil War. Great-grandfather Thomas was captured by the Confederates and sent to Andersonville Prison, of which he was an inmate at least over six months to a year.

The prisoners of that deplorable prison suffered miseries of hunger and thirst, as they had only boards or shacks out on the open ground for protection from the cold or heat and the rain-storms. Their food was of the poorest, usually only corn cob, and oftentimes no water to drink.

Then they were compelled more often to drink from polluted pools on ground, which thru the mercy of God was given the suffering soldiers thru the refreshing showers of rain that fell so mercifully on the sun-baked ground floor of the infamous Andersonville prison. Soon the soldiers became infested with sores on their bodies from the stench that they had endured too long.

Well, as a climax to this true story of the Civil War, Northern and Southern Armies exchanged prisoners six at a time at first, more later on. So one fateful night, in desperation, six of our Civil War veterans, inmates of Andersonville Prison, Great-grandfather included, decided to dig a tunnel under the stone wall of the prison.

Now for the most beautiful ending of our story. A beautiful lady in snow-white garments, supposedly an angel, appeared outside on the brink of a small ravine. She told them they would soon be liberated. She then disappeared.

The following morning, near sunrise, a man came galloping up on a fast horse waving the names of the six prisoners to be exchanged immediately. Great-grandfather was one of the fortunate six included. He lived to a ripe old age, raised a fine family near New Madison, Ohio.

Carrie Pitts Omeara
Wellington, Kansas

"Marching Through Georgia"

I have in my files a letter written on January 22, 1865, by an officer telling of my uncle's capture. He was in Sherman's Army. Part of the letter follows.

"Dear Sir: John was a good and brave soldier. When we were on the march from Atlanta to the coast we were followed very closely by Wheeler's cavalry. (Remember the song, "Marching thru Georgia"?) Near Millidgeville we put up camp, this was on November 25, 1864. Several of our men went out foraging for food on mules. Soon some of the boys came back and said the Rebels had run them and they thought captured some of our boys.

"When John did not return, I was uneasy. About dark his mule came back without him. I knew then that he was captured. I have no reason to think that he was murdered as first reported.

"It is my opinion that you will see him again. But perhaps not until the War is over. I will write again when I learn more.

A Friend, J. Hawkins"

Yes, John came home when the War was over, but he was so thin and sickly his own folks did not know him. He had been forced to live in an open stockade with no roof over his head. His food was one pint of corn chops each day, ground cob and all.

Edith Stukey
Carthage, Missouri

Joyful Reunion For Andersonville Captive

My grandfather was drafted from Indiana early in 1864 into the Union Army. Needless to say, his wife and five tiny girls were heartbroken to see him taken off to war.

He was rushed into battle and within four months was a prisoner in Andersonville Prison. There he languished almost a year, contracting measles, which resulted in losing the sight in one of his eyes.

My mother had the Bible he carried thru the War and on to Andersonville. There were many faded brown spots scattered thruout its pages. Mother explained they were where he smashed the lice he picked from his body. However, he survived the terrible ordeal and was an exchange prisoner. Then he served until the War was over.

Mother has told so vividly of his return. On a chilly, moonlit April night, the mother and five little girls waited from 5 p.m. until 11 p.m. half a mile down the rocky, muddy road for his return home. Mother said the joy of that reunion was almost worth the hardships they had gone thru while he was gone.

Etta Wolter
Fonda, Iowa

Andersonville Memories

Mother used to tell how she listened as a child to the soldiers talking about the comrades they had lost and the hardships they experienced, especially while they were prisoners at Andersonville, where they almost starved to death and suffered a shortage of water, too. She said they would sing the old songs, like "Tenting Tonight on the Old Camp Ground," while tears rained down their faces.

One of the local men, while in prison was in very poor health, and they said he probably would have died had not his cousin, who had the job of feeding the mules, stolen corn from them to give to the sick man. I imagine they roasted it in the ashes, or probably "parched" it in a skillet, in a little fat, if they had any, and then salted it. God took pity on them and a spring broke out in the prison area, and at least they had water to drink. I am not casting any aspersions against their captors, for we all know that soldiers on both sides of the battle line often had to go hungry.

Faye Melton
Lawton, Oklahoma

Escape Tunnel Dug With Butcher Knife

I remember hearing my father tell about his uncle being in prison in a cellar basement during the Civil War, with some more prisoners. Somehow they got hold of an old butcher's knife with the handle off, and they dug a tunnel under a brick wall and a long way with that old knife.

They tamped the loose dirt down in the floor as they dug the tunnel so the guards wouldn't see it. And the night before they were to be killed, they escaped through that tunnel, all but one. He was a large man and he waited till the last one to go, and he got hung in the tunnel and couldn't get all the way through.

Both my grandfathers lost their lives in the Civil War.

Mrs. Adis Ancell
Higbee, Missouri

Too Many Tomatoes

I had a very good friend who was an old soldier of that War. He was captured by Confederate soldiers and taken to Andersonville Prison where he was starved for weeks. He said food was so scarce that their captors were almost as hungry as they were.

Finally he said he was able to escape, and he kept hidden until he was several miles from prison. The first thing he saw that was food was tomatoes growing in quite a large patch. He ate of them until he had all he could eat. And when he got to a place where a

Union soldier took him in, he was certainly sick from eating too many tomatoes.

He never would eat them after that.

Mrs. F. A. Ramel
Beverly, Kansas

Racing To Freedom

I have been told this Civil War story many times by my mother about her father, a young hothead, who was an ardent Southerner and not above a little horse racing and betting on the races.

He was a Confederate soldier and was taken prisoner by the Union soldiers. Grandfather was riding his best saddle mare at the time, a good racing horse.

During the evening while encamped, the talk turned to horses, and Grandfather bragged that his horse could outrun their best horse and challenged his captors to a race, his horse against theirs. The race was to be run a certain distance up around a stake and back to camp.

As the two men rode their horses neck-and-neck to the stake, the Union soldier turned around the stake and headed back to camp but Grandfather whipped his horse and literally flew on past the stake and into the woods and got away from his captors.

Mrs. Rudolph Schmidt
Anselmo, Nebraska

Birth Of A Little Stranger

I can verify what the writer from Kansas wrote concerning the Andersonville Prison during the Civil War.

My father was a soldier in the Civil War and was shot through the arm in the Battle of Gettysburg.

My mother's brother (Uncle Lorenzo) was taken prisoner and placed in the Andersonville Prison. They were so badly in need of good drinking water. Finally a spring of good water broke out in the prison. My uncle was finally set free, but he returned to his family with his health broken and died later.

The heartbreaking point was his wife did not remain true to him, and a little stranger was born in his home.

Harriet Bunch
Newburg, Missouri

Spring Saves Dying Prisoners

My great-grandfather was a Civil War vet enlisted when they lived in West Virginia. He was in the Andersonville Prison when it is said that a spring broke out in the middle of the prison, which supplied water to the prisoners who were dying.

Mahlon Woodley
Jefferson, Iowa

Some Things Stay The Same

Things were very different in the days of the Civil War; they were also much the same. My husband's grandfather and great-grandfather served on the side of the Union.

My husband's grandfather was born in 1842 in Prussia, migrated to America in 1854 with his parents and one brother. At the age of 19 in 1861 he joined the Union Army. He had only been in the States seven years when he enlisted for a period of three years and stated farming as his occupation. He joined for duty at Burlington, Iowa, Co. K, 5th Regiment, Iowa Infantry. Grandfather seemed to have "bad luck" in the Army because he was sick so much. Bad luck is sometimes Good Luck. Because of his hospitalization, he was spared being taken prisoner and being sent to a "Rebel Prison."

In May of 1863 he was wounded at Champion Hills on the march to or during the siege of Vicksburg and sent to the hospital. Shortly thereafter he contracted rheumatism and dysentery from exposure and the Army diet. He was sent to the hospital about the first of August but was back with his regiment by the end of the month. His health continued to fail and he was sent home to recover. He spent from October to spring at his home. Among his papers was an affidavit from his company commander that he was a very sick man.

He was promoted to the Color Guard on his return to his company, which was located at Mission Ridge, Tennessee. When he returned in the spring, he again took ill at Huntsville, Alabama, in June of 1864.

On July 30, 1864, he was mustered out of service as his "tour of duty" was up. He received an honorable discharge.

An interesting side note is that during his last illness, the company was captured and sent to Rebel Prison where the water was contaminated with human waste, food was almost nonexistent and men died by the hundreds.

Grandfather returned home and lived to have a large family, farm and serve in the state legislature.

In 1864 at the age of 38, my husband's great-grandfather was drafted into the Army, reporting to Fort Snelling, Minnesota. The next May he was sent to the hospital at City Point and there the mystery begins. What happened to Great-grandfather, we will never know. City Point was the place where North and South held their prisoner exchange, and reports were that Great-grandfather died on one of the ships taking exchange prisoners from City Point to Washington. There is no evidence that he left the hospital, or got on the boat or of what happened to his body. It can only be surmised that he either wandered away from the hospital, or died on the boat and his body thrown overboard.

Great-grandmother, in an attempt to receive a widow's pension as she was very poor, had much communication from the Pension Office and the Adjutant Office. One office claimed there was no man by Great-grandfather's name in the Army, while the other claimed he had died.

The two offices continued until June of 1881 to voice their different opinions and ask for proof of his service. After this time there is no record of any further communication on the subject. Several men who served with him in the service had come forth in his behalf to state they knew him and had visited with him when he was in the camp hospital at City Point.

How like the modern day Prisoners Of Wars where our soldiers serving and missing in Vietnam cannot be accounted for.

Delores Utecht
Wayne, Nebraska

Chamber Pot Ammunition

My grandfather, William P. Johnson, enlisted in the Confederate Army, May 15, 1861, at Lawrenceburg, Tennessee. He was with the Forrest Calvary Division. According to the testimony of one of his comrades during those trying times, he was one of the bravest of Forrest men.

Grandfather was captured February 16, 1862, at Fort Donelson, Illinois C.S.A. (Confederate States of America). He was in a prisoner exchange seven months later and was appointed corporal at that time. He also accompanied Forrest on scouting trips.

Another time he was the only one captured, and the Yankees put him in a jail cell in a small town. The jail also served as a Yankee hospital and aid station. When a Yankee officer walked in and demanded to see that Rebel, Grandfather picked up the slop jar (chamber pot) from under the cot and hit the officer in the face with its contents. In the ensuing confusion, he got past the guards and back to his own outfit the next day.

Gillie Riley
Rogers, Arkansas

Bartering For A Good Potato

John Jacob Kindscher, my paternal grandfather, came from Switzerland to the United States at age 11 and settled in Iowa. At age 18 he enlisted in the Union Army to fight in the Civil War. He was enrolled as a private in Co. K, 16th Regiment, Iowa Volunteer. The following is taken from his obituary.

"During his active life in the army he enjoyed good health, but he came close to death when returning with a supply of water to his comrades. On finding a wounded Confederate soldier who asked for a drink, Mr. Kindscher stopped to comply with the request. When only a few feet away, the Confederate who was wounded fired at him. This bullet struck the metal part of the U.S. belt he was wearing, which doubtless saved his life."

A short time before entering upon the fourth year of the War, Mr. Kindscher was captured at the Battle of Wilderness while detailed by a commanding officer to procure food for his company and was sent to Andersonville Prison, where he was confined for nine months. His granddaughter, Georgia (Kindscher) Binegar, who compiled the Kindscher Genealogy, wrote the following.

"While at Andersonville, Grandfather Kindscher found a pocket knife that was in good condition. He saw a Confederate guard carrying some potatoes. He asked the guard if he might swap the knife for a good potato. Never had anything tasted as juicy and crisp. This potato seemed to revive Grandfather Kindscher and give him a new zest and incentive to live."

After nine months at Andersonville Prison, because of a break in health, Mr. Kindscher was sent home. As soon as he was physically able, he reenlisted, but the War ended before he reached the Front.

Barbara (Kindscher) Cowgill
Silver Creek, Nebraska

A Pint Of Meal, Cob And All

I have one Civil War story that held me spellbound as a child. My grandfather's oldest brother composed a song and sang it for us. It was a nice tune. but the words have stayed with me all these years.

He was a Union soldier from Illinois and got imprisoned at Andersonville. Their rations were supposed to be one pint of raw cornmeal three times daily, but they held out their hands to get it (not a pint by far), and they lapped it up uncooked.

So he wrote the song and sang it for us. The part I remember so vividly had to do with the cornmeal. Here it is.

What was our daily bill of fare
In this "cecess" saloon?
A pint of meal, ground cob and all
Each morning, night and noon.
Where thousands lay by night and day,
By far too weak to stand,
'Till death relieved their suffering
In Dixie's sunny land.

This "cecess" word may be wrong, but I think it meant secede, like the South did.

Mrs. H. M. Masiella
St. Louis, Missouri

Soldier Survives Terrible Ordeal

This biography is printed on the back of my great-grand-father's picture taken after his recovery. Doctors said he died young (58) because of his treatment in prison.

"In the fall of 1862 the 14th Ill. Cavalry organized in Peoria, and I enlisted in Company B; served until captured on Stoneman's Raid in July 1864, upon retreat from Macon. I was taken by six Rebel soldiers to Andersonville and there kept until the fall of Atlanta made it necessary for us to be removed to prevent our falling in the hands of the Union forces.

"I was taken to Charleston, S. C., with others and placed by the enemy under fire of our soldiers and gunboats; remained here ten days and on or about February 15, I was stricken down by an attack of "swamp fever."

"For three weeks I remained in a delirious condition; the fever abated and reason returned. I soon learned from the surgeon, after a hasty examination, that I was a victim of scurvy and gangrene and was removed to the gangrene hospital.

"My feet and ankles, five inches above the joints, presented a livid, lifeless appearance, and soon the flesh began to slough off, and the surgeon with a brutal oath said I would soon die. But I was determined to live and begged him to cut my feet off, telling him if he would that I could live. He still refused; and believing that my life depended on the removal of my feet, I secured an old pocket knife (I have it now in my possession) and cut through the diseased flesh and severed the tendons. The feet were unjointed, leaving the bones protruding without a covering of flesh of five inches.

"At the close of the War, I was taken by the Rebels to our lines in Wilmington, N. C., in April 1865, and when I weighed learned that I had been reduced from 165 pounds (my weight when captured) to 45 pounds! Every one of the Union surgeons who saw me then said I could not live; but contrary to this belief, I did and improved. Six weeks after release, while on a boat enroute to New York, the bones of my right limb broke off at the end of the flesh. Six weeks later, while in the hospital on David's Island, those of my left had become necrosid and broke off similarly."

"One year after my release, I was just able to sit up in bed and was discharged. Twelve years after my release my limbs had healed over, and strange to relate, no amputation had ever been performed upon them, save the one I had performed in prison. There is no record of any case in the world similar to mine.

Yours, John Wales January"
Mrs. Betty Curtis
Pawnee City, Nebraska

———————■———————

CHAPTER 8: Hard Times At Home

Red Rocker Decoy

The Civil War Centennial brings to mind a tale by my aunt. During the War when Union soldiers were going from house to house taking horses, wagons and food from each family, my aunt's father had put the food under the floors of the house and also in the gutters and in trenches. Then the father crawled under the floor, and the boards were put back by the oldest son.

My aunt was only five years old, but she took her red rocker and sat on a rug over the boards. While the soldiers ate their meal, my aunt sat and rocked on the spot where her father was hiding. My aunt said she could remember the soldiers and the uniforms they wore.

She was 12 when Lincoln was assassinated. She said she was very sad when she saw the mourners' car on the train going to the burial grounds.

Frances Shockey
Atchison, Kansas

Regimental Raids

It seems that there was not much fighting in the home neighborhood, but raids were made to get horses and provisions, which was a common practice in time of war. The soldiers would come to the house, take meat from the smokehouse, also chickens and pigs, or anything they wanted, and then they would order the women on the farms to cook for them. At one place a soldier was carrying a skillet full of fat, and the housewife told him rather sharply not to spill any of it. He assured her he would not even think of doing such a thing, and then turned the skillet upside-down on the well-scrubbed floor.

At one place someone hid some money and valuable things under a plank near a spring. A soldier knelt down to drink, saw the treasure and took it away.

Another tale was told about a farm woman, who upon learning that soldiers were headed her way, took her horses out to the woods and hid them. She was so excited that she forgot where she had tied them, and even with the neighbors helping her, it took several days to find them.

Faye Melton
Lawton, Oklahoma

Everything Must Of Died Around Here

Mother often told us of the hardships they had to endure as the Rebels came through this part of Missouri, not far from where I live today. This was her story.

Father would go hide out in the woods for weeks at a time. He had taken the best horse with him. Each day sister Louise and myself would have to take food and water to him, also some for the horse.

One day, here they came, direct in the house and demanded food. Mother luckily was baking bread, but it was not done. In a gruff voice, they demanded to see it. Mother opened the oven and they said, "Let's have it."

Then they ordered soup plates, broke the bread into it, ordered molasses, which was the only spread people had those days as neighbors would cook that in the fall, poured it over the hot steaming bread and ate it with spoons.

Then Mother and Louise had to go along to the stable or barn. They wanted to know where the boss was, so sister being older said, "He died." "Where is the horse?" they asked. "It's dead." So the reply was, "Everything must of died around here," and they went on.

Mother said that was the happiest day of their life. They were so frightened while they were eating. Their little three-year-old brother was curious and was watching the soldiers the way they were acting and eating.

Finally in a gruff voice one said, "Doesn't that boy ever get anything to eat?" Sister Louise grabbed him and slipped him in another room.

Later in the day we went out to the woods, got Father and all home, but it was a long time before we could feel safe.

E. D. Rohlfing
Berger, Missouri

Raid Leaves Powder Flask

I have heard my father tell many times of General Morgan's raid through Ohio. He was a lad of 10 or 12 years and lived in Ohio where it took place.

General Morgan and his men stopped at my grandfather's to make camp for the night. To feed their horses, they tore the slats off the corn cribs and let the corn roll out on the ground, and the men ate all the food supplies they could find.

When they left the next morning, they took my grandfather with them for several miles, finally turning him loose to make his way back home as best he could.

The next morning my father went out in the yard and found a powder flask (used to load their guns) dropped by one of the men. I have that in my possession now.

We think in horror what our forefathers endured to give us this wonderful country to live in, and we hope and pray there'll never be another war to spill the blood of our young heroes.

Mrs. James K. Whiteaker
Maysville, Missouri

Plenty Of Crust

Grandfather's cousin and her husband lived in southern Indiana and operated a tavern during the Civil War. General Morgan's guerrillas were coming, so her husband took their very fine mare way back and tied her in the brush and came home and hid under the bed. Cousin Mirandy took their money, of which they had considerable, and hid it in her voluminous clothes. General Morgan and his officers came stomping in and ordered her to get dinner. She told them if they wanted dinner to get it themselves. I don't know how good a cook she was, but at least she had plenty of crust.

Glen Smith
Grindley, Kansas

War Makes Devils Of Men

I am reminded of many stories that my grandparents told me. My grandfather fought with the Confederate Army under General Robert E. Lee. For a time, he was a forage master and went to the home of my grandmother's parents in Virginia foraging for food and feed for the horses.

It was during this line of duty that he met my grandmother. They were married the next year, and their little girl was born during the last year of the War.

While my grandmother was lying in bed with the new baby, a young Confederate soldier, who was being pursued by the enemy, went to the home and begged them to hide him. They took him in the room where the young mother and baby were lying and had him hide behind the head of the bed.

Soon the enemy came and demanded entrance to search the house. When they came to the bedroom where the soldier was hiding, my great-grandfather begged them not to enter because there was a young mother who was very ill. The men did not enter Grandmother's room and the young soldier was not captured.

But at another time my great-grandfather's home was visited by a band of soldiers who were just terrorizing people and were not acting under orders. They went to the cellar where there were barrels of cider, molasses, vinegar, coal oil, etc. and opened all of the spigots, letting the contents of all the barrels run together on the floor. They then went up to the kitchen and dining room and picked up stacks of dishes and dropped them to the floor, breaking them.

They took pillows and featherbeds from the house to the yard and ripped them open, letting the feathers fly away in the wind. But their fun ended abruptly for they were caught and shot.

The sad part was the fact that they were neighbor boys, well known to my grandmother's family. So War surely makes devils of men, and they will do things they would not dream of doing under other circumstances.

My grandfather was standing near General Lee when he surrendered. Shortly after the surrender, General Lee turned to my grandfather, whose name was Smith, and said, "Smith, take your horse and go home."

Helen M. Christus
Boonville, Missouri

Half-Hatched Breakfast

An elderly lady in the community was violently pro-Southern in sympathies. But when Yankee soldiers showed up at her house and demanded breakfast, she had to agree. She proceeded to cook scrambled eggs (taken from under the hens and containing half-hatched chicks).

After calling the men, she went and locked herself in the cellar. Years later, one of the diners attended her church regularly. It is said that he was never able to look her in the eye without turning a pale green and covering his lips with a hanky!

Elaine Derendinger
New Franklin, Missouri

Featherbed Sandwich

While Grandfather was fighting in the War, he hid out in all kinds of places to escape capture. But eventually he was captured and held prisoner for quite some time. While he was imprisoned, the enemy entered the home where Grandma and the five small children were waiting for him to come back. They took many things, including all of their bed covers and their supply of cured meat, hidden in the attic.

Grandma put all the children to bed on one featherbed and covered them up with another.

His family, as well as he, endured many hardships, not knowing whether he would ever come back to them or not.

Mrs. James F. Kidwell
Clarence, Missouri

Diaper Pail Protection

My grandfather (on my father's side) went to the War for the North, leaving a wife and children, my father being the baby. My grandmother's sister, Poppy, had one of the finest horses, saddle and bridle in the country and served as messenger and carried the mail. She was on such a mission when the Rebels caught sight of her and were going to take her horse, saddle and bridle away from her. She gave them the rap of the whip across their hands and swiftly down the road she flew, arriving home just in time to hide the bridle and saddle under a pile of my father's soiled diapers. When the Rebels drove in and began searching for it, one of them stopped by the pile of diapers. Aunt Pop said, "Oh, I guess you don't want those; they're just Warren's soiled diapers." He turned his head and grinned, but walked away. Well, that's all that saved her gear that time!

Another time, Grandmother said they were all ready to sit down to the noon meal when in came a troop of Rebels. Without saying a word they came in, seated themselves at the table, rested their rifles across their laps and ate their dinner, not leaving a crumb. After eating they went out to the smokehouse and rolled away all their barrels of meat.

My other grandmother and her sister lived together while their husbands were away. One day while they were gone, the Rebels came and piled out all of Aunt Ellen's things and Grandmother's; all went up in smoke. Of course, Aunt Ellen's husband was fighting for the South, otherwise they wouldn't have known Grandma's things from Aunt Ellen's.

The Civil War was a long hard war, but Grandpa lived through it alright but died a few years later with the flu, right beside Grandma, and she didn't even know it at the time.

Mrs. John Feek
Morrill, Kansas

Saved By The Well

A cousin has told me the story of how her family's silver and precious keepsakes were saved from the Union soldiers by their faithful Negro servant, Adam.

Word was sent by a neighbor's young Negro houseboy, who sneaked through the woods to their home to warn them that the Union soldiers were foraging, and so they had a little time to hide things.

All the silverware, any jewelry they had and other keepsakes that they felt the Union soldiers might take were hastily dumped into a large, dark-colored bag that had a draw cord in the top and a rope tied to the draw cord. Uncle Adam, the faithful Negro servant, suspended it down into the well by the long rope and concealed the rope tied around the support for the windlass as best he could.

The Union soldiers arrived and took the chickens, and some other things, but when they went through the house, they couldn't seem to find anything of value to them.

When the soldiers stopped at the well to draw up a bucket of cold water, the hearts of the watching family were in their throats, but by good fortune they didn't notice the rope suspended into the well, or else thought it was merely something put down in the well to be kept cold, as was the custom, and so the family treasures were saved.

Estelle Laughlin
Gering, Nebraska

Slop Jar Molasses

My grandfather fought in the War, leaving behind his wife and several small children.

It is well known how the Armies had to forage for food. One day a runner came to my grandmother's home saying word had come that an Army was coming, taking any food which they could find.

My grandmother, with the help of the children, began taking all food they could inside the house. A large wooden barrel filled with molasses was too heavy to be moved.

The Army, of course, found the barrel, but it was too heavy and bulky to take along so they began looking for a container in which to take part of the molasses. The only thing available was an old stone crock, which grandmother, having no slop jar, had used for the family so she would not have to take her children outside at night when they had to go to "the restroom." She had placed it outside to sun.

Being ignorant of its use, they filled the crock with molasses and went on their way.

I can still picture my grandmother as she told the story and laughed until tears ran down her cheeks.

Rosell Kirk
Seneca, Missouri

The Last Silver Spoon

Among my dearest keepsakes is a little silver spoon bearing the letter "C" engraved on the handle. This was given to me by a dear old auntie who told me the story. Her mother's silver had the letter "C" engraved on each piece, and it was a treasured possession.

One day two Union soldiers, who were out foraging, stopped and demanded something to eat. She prepared a meal for them, and the soldiers sat down at the dining table and ate.

Later, as they left, it was observed that their pockets were sagging, and as they swung up on their horses, there was a jangling noise. It was soon discovered that the jangling noise came from my grandmother's silver, which they had taken from the sideboard. Only one lone spoon was overlooked, and it was prized by my grandmother, who often spoke with regret of her lost silver.

When they moved North, Grandmother Lucie Belle never failed to note the silverware in any home where she happened to be, but she never found her long lost silver. The one spoon has been passed down through the generations, and today is displayed in a spoon rack with other cherished pieces.

Estelle Laughlin
Gering, Nebraska

Even Skunk Tasted Good

Talk about Civil War days. I can still remember the one most interesting story in which my great-uncle played a part. He used to tell how they got hungry and cooked a skunk for meat and how good it tasted. He used to say, "that when you get darn good and hungry, you can eat most anything."

Virgil Elstermeier
Marquette, Nebraska

Carpet Rags Camouflage

The Loverchecks lived in Missouri, where both North and South soldiers passed through. As was the custom, both groups searched every home and took anything that appealed to them.

One of their neighbors prepared for the soldiers by stringing barrels of carpet rags all over their house, both upstairs and down. When the first group of soldiers saw the mess, they didn't even want to go inside, but just cussed and said the other side had beaten them to that home.

Another incident happened when the soldiers took the folks' only team and left them a sick mare and a great big old stubborn mule. The girls, as the boys had gone to fight, had a terrible time harnessing and getting the crops in the ground. When it came time to cultivate or plow the corn, that ornery old mule stepped on the corn rows all the time. So the harvest was very small that fall. Those times were very grim, but the antics of that old mule were funny years later.

Ruth Williamson
Gering, Nebraska

Warning Saves Family And Food

Great-grandmother was only 13 when the Civil War started. The family lived in the foothills of the Great Smoky Mountains in East Tennessee. Times were hard, and with the menfolk gone off to war, it was about all my great-grandmother could do to rustle up enough food for her five children.

In the years gone by, Great-grandfather had cleared enough ground for a hillside garden and land for what corn and wheat his family would need to see them through until the next season.

One day a neighbor boy came running down the toe-path, bringing word that the soldiers were headed in that general direction. Great-grandmother sent my grandmother to round up the cow and oxen and drive them into the woods.

Great-grandmother gathered all the available food, then she and the four younger children hurried into the woods to find my grandmother. They stayed hid out until they were sure the soldiers were gone.

They were thankful the warning came in time for them to hide the stock. Many families in their locality did not fare as well, because the hungry soldiers slaughtered their stock for food.

Adeline Ferguson
San Diego, California

Grandma's Quick Thinking

During the Civil War my great-grandparents lived in the mountains of Virginia. Grandpa was called to serve in the Army, leaving Grandma almost alone, except for a small son. Times were hard for Grandma. She had to do her own work, including getting her own wood.

A railroad was built through the countryside and was left unfinished. Railroad ties were plentiful, so Grandma took advantage of unused ties, rolling them down the mountain, thus using them for firewood. An old man, who was too old for Army service, helped her get wood when it was snowy.

Soldiers came through the countryside, raiding homes and taking anything they wanted. Grandma's parents lived on a crossroads, operating a tavern. It had been ransacked by soldiers before Grandma visited them, so when Grandma went to visit, she knew they were without food, and she carried the bag of cornmeal along.

On arriving she found the soldiers there. As Grandma wore a full-skirted dress, she proceeded to sit on the meal and remained there until the soldiers left. They also went upstairs and came down with fresh white shirts, which had been stored away.

Frances Gump
Clarksburg, Missouri

Wives, Mothers And Heroines

Many soldiers suffered in that War, enduring hardships such as long marches without sufficient clothing or food.

It is true the Generals planned and executed the War strategy, altho' the mothers and wives at home wrote the lines of that epic struggle. For example, my mother was one of those who was left on a farm with two babies. My father volunteered in the struggle as his brother-in-law promised to look after my mother. However, this brother-in-law failed to keep his promise.

She would leave the older one (who could sit on the floor and play) with a pan of water to play in, while she carefully placed the baby safely back on the bed, while she did the outside work such as feeding stock and chickens, milking the cow and getting in her fuel.

We are thankful that our boys and their families are better cared for now.

Herman Clark
Winchester, Kansas

It Wasn't Squirrel For Lunch

During the Civil War, living in Texas as a small 12-year-old boy, my father went to play with a neighbor widow's two boys.

At noon the lady called them in to eat lunch, which consisted of fried meat and bread, which he enjoyed. In the middle of the afternoon, she called again to the boys to go kill some more rats for their evening meal.

My father's appetite quickly disappeared for the squirrel he had eaten at noon, so he went home.

Mrs. Paul Boyd
Ardmore, Oklahoma

Rebel Bees

Uncle Alex was in the Southern Army until one day he was standing near a cannon when it exploded, causing deafness; blood ran from eyes, ears and nose. A deaf man was useless in the Army. He was sent home, honorably discharged. He remained so until the end of the War. The family and others thought he could hear, that he was fighting against right, and used his deafness to good advantage. Many tried, in different ways, to prove he could hear by making loud noises near, etc., but he was deaf to all sounds and the family never knew for sure anything different. They only knew that after the War closed, his hearing returned.

Grandpa Cato and Uncle Alex voted against the secession of the Southern states, but they had to fight with the South when war was declared. They could never quite forget how the Yankees came through their country, destroying their property, shooting their stock, etc.

They had a large colony of bees, the Yankees came by one day when Aunt Belle happened to be in the house alone. The soldiers decided they would help themselves to some honey, but the bees were Rebels. They came out of the hives and swarmed over those Yankees, stinging them furiously. The bees won their battle. And how Aunt Belle laughed at the Yankees' discomfiture. When her family heard how she had laughed, they thought she was very foolish.

By Elsie Surbaugh
Submitted by
Althea Fifield Kendall
Pullman, Washington

Comely Girls Create Diversion

My grandmother often told the following story to her children and grandchildren about an incident during the Civil War.

Papa went to Camden, Arkansas, to declare his allegiance to the South and enlist. They didn't take him into the Army, because he was too old and also had weak wrists. The soldiers took him to work in a saddle shop.

One day a neighbor came riding in to tell us the Confederate Army was on its way through that part of the country. He said the soldiers were living off the areas through which they went, buying and stealing.

The family scurried to take the horses and cows into the woods and to hide their supply of food. Some was hidden up the flue, put on the roof and in other places hidden from the approaching Army.

The Army arrived late in the afternoon. Mama refused to sell the soldiers any food, so they ransacked the house and barn, taking whatever they could find. The troops prowled around and took the livestock and poultry.

While the Army camped nearby, soldiers were stationed at both entrances of the house to protect the family. My sisters Sarah and Mary flirted with the guards and gave them plates of food after we had eaten. After the War, one of them returned and married Sarah.

When one of the soldiers began to search in the trunks, Mama knew he was looking for the deed to the farm. His attention was diverted when Sarah and Mary walked into the room and smiled at him. Mama reached into the trunk, quickly putting the deed into her deep apron pocket.

Betty J. French
Mercedes, Texas

Hard Life In Tragic Times

I am enclosing an account of my ancestors in southeast Missouri during the Civil War.

When my great-great-uncle, Andrew Martin Bugg, hiked from Patterson, Missouri, to Union City, Tennessee, to enlist in the Confederate Army on July 22, 1861, at the age of 21, the family he left behind undoubtedly suffered nearly as much hardship as he.

Martial law was declared in Wayne County, Missouri, on August 3, less than two weeks after Andrew arrived in Union City.

Shortly after hostilities started, Missouri Governor Jackson immediately organized a Home Guard throughout the state, supposedly to repel both Union and Confederate forces. The North interpreted it as an act of war, and reinforcements of Union troops chased the Home Guard into Arkansas. Residents of Wayne County were under a constant struggle to survive throughout the War. The Union soldiers would commit atrocities, then the former Home Guard would ride across the border from Arkansas and retaliate. Pillaging went on from both sides.

My great-great-grandparents lived on a farm outside of Patterson, just about three miles from Fort Benton, a Union fort. During a Union foray, my great-great-grandparents spotted the Union soldiers coming and hid the silver and some large portraits in the oven.

It was a chilly day and the soldier in charge insisted the stove be lit. Whether it was a clever ploy on the part of the soldier for amusement as he watched their faces as the oven grew warmer, or merely from the cold is not known. Finally, either sufficiently warmed, or satisfied there was nothing in the oven, the soldiers departed, but not before the portraits were badly charred.

This was minor compared to real suffering that went on in Wayne County. Men of Southern extraction had to stay in hiding, livestock was taken, homes burned and families exiled. Many men remaining at home joined the Enrolled Missouri Militia just to stay alive and keep families from being persecuted.

One Union report relating a typical scouting expedition which took place just two months after martial law was proclaimed, sums it up well: "having been out 6 days, marched 145 miles, killed 10 men, burned 23 houses, captured 15 horses and mules....all of which is respectfully submitted."

That particular Union lieutenant had grown up in Wayne County and knew all the residents. He knew the names of all the men shot, the first three who were just walking on the road, and named the owners of the houses he burned, saying he knew them to be Rebels and bushwhackers.

Barbara Farber
Canon City, Colorado

A Different View of Cole Younger

Not as much has been said or written about the Border Wars as about the Civil War. And yet, the two are a part of each other. The fighting along the Kansas-Missouri line was cruel and bloody. William Clark Quantrill was a guerrilla warfare leader in this area and had among his followers such outlaws as the James Brothers and Cole Younger and his band.

Quantrill and his men were causing such havoc along the border that General Ewing issued Order No. 11, the gist of which meant swift and cruel punishment to anyone harboring Confederate soldiers. In this region it was hard to tell who leaned toward the Union and who leaned toward the Confederacy.

The story comes down through my husband's family of an unusual incident that happened about this time. Cole Younger took a chance when he knocked on the door of this farmer, asking for a place for his band of men to camp. They needed to rest, eat and sleep he told the farmer.

This man stood in the door looking at the band of rough-looking men. What was he to do? If he said they could stay, he might be turned in as a Confederate sympathizer. If he told them they couldn't stay, there was no telling what might happen. He silently assessed the situation and decided for the sake of his family, he must tell them they could stay. However, in return, he extracted a promise from Cole that no one in his family would be harmed.

When the farmer started to tell Cole where he should camp, Cole informed the farmer he had already checked out the situation and had found the perfect place to camp. A spring, feeding into a creek with tall trees and brush, which would hide his men from prying eyes, would be the right site.

Instead of an overnight stay, the men camped there several nights. Needless to say, there was not much sleeping being done inside the house.

When Cole came to the door a few mornings later, he politely thanked the farmer for letting them stay. He talked about the wonderful spring water and the comfortable area where they slept. When he finished talking, he handed the owner some money to pay for the trouble he had caused. He told the man he hoped their stay would not bring suspicion to the household. He and his men disappeared down the road.

Zoe Rexroad
Adrian, Missouri

A Brave Woman's Graveyard Raid

Elizabeth Ann Oberchain had much to worry about that summer in 1864. When word came that General Hunter's Army was marching with a large Army up the Valley of Virginia to attack Lynchburg from the rear, Elizabeth Ann was especially worried. Her eldest son, (who was serving in the Confederate Army), had left at home some eight or 10 pounds of sporting powder.

When Hunter's advance guard appeared on the opposite side of the river from Buchanan, Mrs. Obershain, fearing that her house would be searched by federal soldiers as soon as they entered the town. Wishing to save her son's powder, she carried it over to the churchyard of St. John's, which adjoined her premises. She concealed it under some rank, matted grass near an old tombstone in the rear of the church, where from the solemnness of the place, she supposed no soldier would go, and that the powder would be safe.

Great then was her surprise and amazement when, going out on the back porch at about 10 p.m., she saw several fires burning in that part of the churchyard and soldiers lying around them on the ground. She realized at once the situation. "Should fire get to that powder," she thought, "and cause it to explode and do any injury, the soldiers, supposing it was intentional, would become infuriated and burn the town." The mere thought of being the cause of such a calamity, though innocent, was more than she could bear.

Followed by her housemaid, Hannah, she went out through the garden and crept cautiously up to the dividing fence. Soldiers were stretched out on the ground here and there on the other side, fast asleep. Some of the fires were spreading slowly into the grass.

Thinking not of self — not of her own danger, but only of what might happen to others — she whispered to Hannah to remain where she was, climbed the fence noiselessly, crept steadily among the sleeping soldiers, got the powder and returned safely with it to the house.

When told afterward that she was in great peril at the time; that if she had been detected when coming out with the powder in her possession, the soldiers would have believed she was attempting to do the very thing she had gone there to prevent, she replied, "I did not once think of that."

Mrs. Morris Borden Tucker
Oklahoma City, Oklahoma

From The Pen Of A Contemporary

"Oh, I wonder if it is as plain in other people's memories that were living in those days as it is in mine, of, the happy days before the War when my brothers and sisters and I were home on the mountain farm with our father and mother.

My father had a farm of 160 acres, all under good tillage. But, oh, when the War broke out and the cry came for soldiers. My father and my two brothers were scarcely young men grown, as were our three hired farm hands. But when the call came, the five left home and enlisted. It was in the midst of haying time, leaving my father without a soul to help him.

Then it was that my dear mother and I had to take a hand out of doors. There were no mowing machines at that time or horse rakes. At that time, father mowed the grass by hand with a scythe. It fell my lot to turn the grindstone to grind that scythe. Sometimes I thought my arms would break before the grinding was done. When father mowed the grass, I had to follow with a pitch fork and spread it out to dry. Then after dinner Father, Mother and I would all fall to and rake it into windrows. Then Father would get the horses and big wagon and he would hitch the wagon and I made load and Mother raked after. Then when the load was made, Father would drive on to the barn floor. I on top of the load would get on the scaffold and mow it away. I, only a weak girl of 15 years, but Father could not get help for love nor money. In the midst of this my father was taken sick. He had worked too hard.

We had finished the haying but it was clear along in September and the harvesting was to be done with no one but my mother and myself, beside two small boys, my brothers, that were of very little use. We had very large fields of potatoes to dig and turnips. I remember it so well, we had 170 bushels of turnips and such a quantity of potatoes. I can't tell how many, but I can remember the number of bushels of turnips because when I pulled them, I gave the little boys two cents a bushel for cutting off the tops.

Until that time I had never milked a cow. Mother knew how, but she had not milked for years. She had to take a hand at it and she taught me how, for we had a large dairy of cows, and we were making a great deal of butter at the time.

Father also had a large hoghouse full of hogs that had to be cured and large fields of oats. I had a 10 dollar gold piece, the first one I ever saw. I gave it to a man for cutting or cradling the oats; I raked and bound them. We could not get anyone to thrash them, so we fed them out in with straw. Oh, those were hard times. But we had enough to eat, that which we raised upon the farm."

By Minna (Fowler) Rounds
Submitted by Paul H. Rounds
Severance, Kansas

"Play Party" For Departing Soldiers

Grandmother was a young lady of 16 in 1861. She passed along memories of those traumatic times to her youngest son.

She told of a star formation that appeared as a great "W" in the sky. In those days, people were very superstitious. It is likely they saw what they wanted to see. Everyone took it as a sign that a great war threat hung over the land.

Grandmother told about the many things they experimented with as coffee substitutes. Coffee was scarce, and when it was available, it was too expensive to afford. They parched corn or other grains and baked them until nearly black before it was ground and boiled for ersatz coffee. They even tried roasted acorns, but those needed much soaking and leaching to remove the bitter acids from the final drink.

She mentioned the lack of good flour. The best flour was sent to the Army. They struggled to make edible breads from less desirable grains. Corn pones or journey cake made with coarse cornmeal, water and no leavening was a mainstay in their daily fare.

Many community young men were leaving to join the Union forces. Their young friends decided to have a last "play party" to honor them. The girls made great preparations, combining all the goodies they could manage to hoard for gingerbreads, corn cakes, molasses and sugar cookies and vinegar sling to drink.

They held their party at the largest home available, where they sang and danced to old-time folk tunes and sing-song games. A zealous minister heard about the party and broke it up with exhortations against their sinful playing. Because of that, Great-grandfather vowed never to attend that church again.

Grandmother was an expert stocking and mitten knitter. She made countless pairs to send to friends and relatives in the Army. Her clothing was all stitched by hand, and all worn garments were taken apart, turned wrong side out and resewn to look newer.

The best parts of worn clothing were cut up and stitched again into children's clothes or into quilts. New fabrics were so scarce and very expensive during the War, so Grandmother learned to save the smallest scraps and piece them together to finish one tiny quilt patch.

A young man from the neighborhood was badly wounded on the Chickamauga battlefield. He found shelter in a brush patch and waited for several days to be found and given medical attention.

A treasured memento of those agonizing days was a ring he had whittled from a root to while away the long painful hours of dreary waiting.

Jean Kristiansen
Nashua, Iowa

Grandfather Smith's Memories

Our grandfather, Martin L. Smith, lived with his children several years before his death in 1939. While he was in our parents' home, my sister and I were often reminded of Grandpa's childhood in Maryland as he reminisced.

Mart, as he was familiarly known, was a lad of eight or nine years, living in Maryland's Washington County when the armies of the Blue and the Gray were encroaching his father Solomon Smith's farm on Elk Ridge Mountain in Pleasant Valley not far from Rohrersville. Troops (Confederate or Union ?, both traveled the area) converged and looted his family's mountainside home during confrontations at Antietam in September 1862 and during the advance to and retreat from Gettysburg in mid-1863.

One incident was that the family was forced to leave the home, the house was ransacked, and belongings and personal effects were taken. When they returned, the Northern Army shared bedding and food until the family could stock up again. Another encounter was the use of the little farmhouse as a temporary infirmary, and this curious youngster peeking through a window witnessing amputation of a limb from a wounded soldier.

To escape troops marching to or retreating from Gettysburg, his mother, Sophia, took refuge up the side of the mountain and got lost in a briar thicket. She struggled for an hour or so before reaching a clearing. Three-month-old daughter, Emma, was carried in her arms, six-year-old Sam and nine-year-old Mart held onto her skirts.

Helen C. Dingler
Enterprise, Kansas

Soldiers Were Frequent Visitors

Susan Elizabeth James and her twin sister, Rachel, were born September 8, 1847, in Georgia. The family moved to Tennessee when the girls were eight years old. At the age of 18, they married brothers, both Civil War veterans. Susan Elizabeth married Anderson Putman, who fought for the South, and Rachel married John Royner Putman who fought for the North.

The James family lived in a two-story brick house on a plantation in Jefferson County, Tennessee. While some of the battles were fought near their home, the Union soldiers frequented their home, carrying off chickens, cows, hogs and anything they wanted or could use. Salt, a necessity, was $18 a pound. Those who could not afford to buy salt boiled the dirt from the floor of the smokehouse and drained the water for the salt. Calico was the most expensive material to buy; Susan paid $22 for calico material to make a dress after the War.

By Effie Slater
Submitted by Margaret Kenyon
Guthrie, Oklahoma

Ties That Bind

Though my mother was born after the Civil War, this War had affected her life and the lives of all those around her. Mother was a great one for keeping alive memories of her childhood.

At the age of seven she was left an orphan, both parents dying of pneumonia, a very common occurrence then. The eldest of five children, she was sent to live with her mother's parents, who owned a large plantation in Kentucky. Thirty years after the War now, Grandfather was getting old, older than his years would warrant, but his life and livelihood had been shattered by the Great War.

Though he had not fought in the Great War, he, nevertheless, had felt the full force of its destruction. He still had his land, but no workers to help him plant the many acres. His livestock had been requisitioned by the military, and all he had left was one old mule, Jake. He had managed to get a cow and some chickens; these along with his garden, supplied them with food.

Grandfather had always grown tobacco and this is a work intensive crop. He had put in a few acres by himself with only the help of his three teenaged daughters and now his granddaughter. They all had to work in the fields, hoeing, picking off tobacco worms, cutting the crop when it was ready and carting it to the barn for drying. Even at this time of shortage of men to do the field work, it was considered "common" for a woman to work in the fields.

To hide the fact that they did work outside, the four girls wore long-sleeved, long dresses and big bonnets on their heads. If anyone was heard coming down their road, the girls would make a beeline for the barn and stay hidden until the visitors would leave. After a day's work in the fields, the girls would wash up at the hand pump outside and then apply buttermilk to their skin to bleach out any suntan or freckles. A smooth white skin was a prerequisite for a lady. Working this way, the family somehow eked out an existence, though it was far from the one they had known in years past.

My mother married young, had a large family and for many years lived in the South. At one point my two oldest brothers bought a newspaper to run "up North," not far from Chicago. So, we all moved north. For the first time in our lives we attended integrated schools and churches. Strangely enough an elderly Negro man, known as Daddy James, also lived in this community. The moment he heard we were in town, he came to visit. Almost unbelievably, he had been a small boy on my grandfather's farm and still remembered him well. When he saw my mother he cried, he was so happy to see her.

He told us many stories about how much he had loved my grandfather and how good Grandfather had been to him. After that he came to us often, bringing his fiddle and playing music for us and reminiscing with my mother and father about the "oldendays."

141

Daddy James had lived up north for many years, but he still kept his courtly Southern ways. One day when he was leaving our house, I decided I would like to walk to town with him. (I was only seven at the time) and I really thought a lot of Daddy James. But he gently shook his head and told me I could not walk with him. "But why, Daddy James?" I asked. "Because, child, it just wouldn't be seemly," he replied.

I remember standing there on the sidewalk, puzzled at his answer. I didn't understand him, but I respected him.

The Civil War has not been forgotten, you know, but the links between people who lived during that time, or knew people who experienced that War, are now very few. How grateful I am to have been able to be one of those links.

Helen Ward O'Key
Litchfield, Connecticut

CHAPTER 9: Letters To Loved Ones

Esteemed Officer Falls

The following letter was written on May 18, 1863, to my great-grandmother, informing her of the death of her husband, my great-grandfather, Captain William Carbee. Captain Carbee was killed in the battle of Champion Hill, Mississippi, on May 16, 1863.

Edwards Station, Mississippi

It becomes my painful duty to inform you that on the 16th, our worthy Captain and your beloved husband fell on the Bloody field of battle while nobly and bravely leading his gallant Company in one of the most desperate charges (on a Battery of five guns) which had been made during the War.

He was struck by a ball in the Right breast, which killed him instantly. I was by his Side when he fell. Our, as well as your, loss is irreparable. His Kindness and affection and Promptness in the discharge of his duty not only won for him the admiration and esteem of his own company, But of the whole Regiment.

When we get possession of Vicksburg, if the authorities will permit, I will have him taken up and sent home, as it was his request, and doubtless it will be a great source of comfort to you. I will write to John Carbee as soon as we stop.

Yours truly,
A. R. Knott, 1st Lieutenant
Alice Stewart
Cedar Rapids, Iowa

Note From A Loving Husband

The following is from a letter written October 4, 1863, from Matthia Wilson to his wife, Ruth Mosher Wilson, in West Liberty, Iowa.

Camp Near Black River
Oct. 4, 1863

My dear wife,

This is a beautiful Sabbath day and I thought I would spend part of it writing to thee. I received thy letter of the eighteenth last evening. I think one of thy letters has been miscarried. The last one that I received before last evening was written on the sixth. That was a long time to me without hearing from thee, my own loving companion.

How heavily the time passes when we are expecting to get a letter from the loved one and are disappointed. Days appear almost as long as weeks did when we were living so happily together. I often think of those days and wonder if we will live to see as happy days again.

I expect we will have to move again soon. I expect we will be moving back toward Vicksburg. The guerrillas are getting bold. They shot a Lieutenant of our Division last Thursday night while on picket, and Joseph Alger came very near being taken prisoner yesterday. He was about one mile and a half from camp and four Rebels came very near catching him.

I am enjoying pretty good health now. I was very glad to hear that thee and our little ones was well. Please excuse this short letter as I have a piece of poetry that I want to copy and send to thee that I think is much better than anything I could write.

I am perfectly satisfied with the way thee is managing our affairs. I am very near out of pocket handkerchiefs.

As ever, Thy loving husband
Matt Wilson
Lena Ruth Hampton
Palisade, Colorado

Letter Of Brotherly Love

Enclosed is a copy of one of my most cherished keepsakes — a Civil War letter. George Wineman wrote it to his little sister Margaret (later my mother) when he was a Union soldier in the War. George made the supreme sacrifice July 2, 1863, during the Battle of Gettysburg.

At the top of the Union stationery, on which the letter is written, is an appropriate illustration in colors: in the left background the sky is dark and ominous over tempestuous waters; fierce barbs of lightning pierce a sinking Confederate ship, flying a pitifully tattered flag. In the right background is a Union ship sailing smoothly in tranquil waters under a clear, calm sky. In the center foreground is the Stars and Stripes and a dauntless eagle firmly established on a firm, huge rock.

I have typed the letter just as it was written, with misspelled words, no paragraphing and very little punctuation.

Camp near Warrington
July the 10th, 1862

Dear Sister,

I take this favourable opertunity of informing you that I am well, and hope these few lines may find you enjoying the same and all the rest. I was looking for a letter for three or four days, for it is a good while since I wrote Dave and Paps, but I received your letter today with the thread and neadles and a good bit of writing. You want to know what them hooks are for, well, for my part I never saw any use made of them, but I think if you look right you will see a couple of eyes on the front of the coat tail and them hooks can be hooked into them and made a kind of shad belly of it, or whatever you may call it. Well, I know nothing about Harrison Wetherow, yet you say the cherrys are getting ripe. Well, they are about done here. I eat a great many cherrys and a wonderful lot of blackberrys, that is the low ones, it beatz all for fruit in Virginia. You ought to see the peaches, the trees just hanging full, and pears and apples are plenty. Butter is cheap in our valley, I must say if you had it here you could make money. It was 30 cents a pound when I bought mine and I heard it was 50 cents now. We are a good piece in Virginia now and we are under martching order. We may martch tomorrow. We need not buy that funy kind of supe, we get meat three times a day. Today we got pork salt beef and good fresh beef and got sugar and molasses. I bought corn bread today for only 10 cents — worth it, it was a good bit and it is good. I bought a good big thick peach pie one day for 25 cents. We will be paid soon and then I am going to send by expres forty dollars for old dad to make use of. I'll trust him, I don't care how long. Well if I get a chance to get my likeness taken I will, but I am too far away from Washington to go there. What is the reason that unkle samuel did not get his letter? I don't know for I wrote it before yours. I must bring my letter to a close, no more at present but remain your loving Brother, G. B. Wineman. Direct the same as before (we gained great victorys at Richmond).

Mrs. J. F. Neaderhiser
Longford, Kansas

Lonesome And Sick

Grandfather was a Confederate soldier who was taken prisoner. I have a drawing of the prison at Rock Island where he was. It was made by a fellow prisoner and dated 1863. Following are excerpts from letters which Grandfather wrote home to his family.

Meridian, Mississippi, Jan. 2, 1863: I am tolerable well. We heard there had been a fight at Murfreesboro, Tenn., and we had taken 16,000 prisoners and 30 cannon. I hope it is so."

Vicksburg, Mississippi, Feb. 7, 1863: We have had no fight here yet. The enemy is camped on the other side of the river. There was one gunboat went down the river. We shot at it like everything, but she went ahead. We haven't much chance with their gunboats. Provisions are powerful high. Pork without salt is worth 50 and bacon one dollar. Corn very high. I heard yesterday there had been another fight at Murfreesboro, and we whipped them. The talk is that the Yanks are leaving here going to re-inforce Rosencrans.

Vicksburg, Misssissippi, Feb. 27, 1863: Times is as hard as you ever heard of. We are getting beef and corn bread, but the best kind of beef is so poor it reels as it walks. The corn is just hominy. There is nothing to sell and what there is is so high a private can't buy anything to eat. Bacon is one dollar per pound, potatoes four dollars a bushel, chickens two dollars a piece and eggs a dollar twenty-five a dozen.

The Yanks sent one boat down the river, and we took it about the mouth of the Red River and then they sent another one, and the one we had captured of theirs and another one of ours got after it and sunk it and took all the men. There was twelve guns on the two boats."

Vicksburg, Mississippi, April 14, 1863: I have been sick about five weeks. I can just go about the camp. For about three weeks I could not go about at all. The boys waited on me the best they could but there is nothing a sick person can eat. The Yanks are still over the river. There is some cannonading occasionally. Tell the boys to work hard at home. Now is the time one man at home can make as much as ten in the army. I am very lonesome and sick.

Rock Island, Illinois, Oct. 24, 1864: I have been here eleven months. I seen a very hard time. It is the worst part of my life so you can guess what kind of fare we have in prison. Some of the Roane County boys have joined the Union Army. I will give you their names.

Among his letter and paper is one from the Secretary of War granting a leave to paroled prisoners at Richmond, Virginia, March 12, 1865.

When he was a very old man, Grandfather was spry enough to dance a jig when they played "Dixie."

James E. Hall
Lamar, Colorado

Love To All My Friends

I have in my possession a letter, yellowed with age, written January 5, 1863, in very fine handwriting, by my grandfather at Lexington, Kentucky, to my grandmother at Louden City, Illinois. I would love to share every bit of it with you, but as it is such a long letter I will send the last paragraph. Here it is.

Write soon in answer to this for I have not received my pay yet and I have been informed that they will only pay us 1 1/2 months pay this time. That will only be nineteen dollars and 50 cents, leaving twenty-six dollars unpaid. Pray for me that I may be brought safely through my trouble and meet you in heaven. Give my love to all my friends.

> Farewell for the present.
> Joseph Beck to Lydia and Family
> Mrs. John Patterson
> Krebs, Oklahoma

Father's Report To Daughter

This letter is from a fourth cousin of mine that was a Methodist minister, and was made a Captain in the Union Army. He was later killed in action.

> Camp Near Lexington, Kentucky
> Nov. 6, 1862

Dear Daughter,

I have been thinking for some time about answering your letter. It was received and contents noted in due time.

I am in pretty good health. My throat is a little sore from cold and talking so much.

We will drill five hours each day, Sunday excepted, spend one hour at guard mounting and one hour at Dress or evening Parade so you see that I put in Seven hours at work. One hour is spent in eating breakfast, dinner and supper, reports take up another hour, making in all on the part of the officers nine hours per day. But so little time is given to spend in idleness even if we were disposed to do so. Today there are three Captains and one Lieutenant put under arrest and their swords taken away from them. Capts. Lapham, Williams and Hays. I do not remember the Lieut. They were arrested for disobeying a general order which requires all commissioned officers to report themselves in person at the Regimental Headquarters every morning at five and a half o'clock. Lieut. Bridgewater was placed under Guard for four hours for suffering one man to break ranks while marching. I believe that nearly every officer of the Regiment has been, or should be, arrested.

So far I have gotten along without much difficulty. We have a pretty jolly set of men down here, about thirty thousand in all, I believe. There is little of interest in our midst.

I believe so far as I can learn that there is not fighting going on, all though of this you know better than I. We get but little news out here, sometimes we don't see a paper for ten days, and sometimes we see them every day. I believe on the whole we are gaining ground all the time. Our Armies seem to be gradually moving forward toward the enemy and the enemy retreating the meanwhile. If you ask when this war will cease and harmony prevail again, I answer when the Nation repents in dust and ashes, then the thing will cease, and not until then.

My prayer is that the day may hasten when all will fall down and earnestly repent of all their sins individually and Nationally, but as to when the Nation will see the folly of their course, I cannot say. But one thing is certain, I can see no other way of safety before me by which I can gain a home in Heaven, and therefore I feel a holy resolve to travel in that way. The best way and easiest to get along through this world is the path of duty, and as an intelligent man I want to go in that way. Daughter, you must be religious and make your way to Heaven.

Old Father Hymer on the Rushville circuit is dead and gone to Heaven.

Just now I learn that the Rebels have taken Nashville, Tennessee.

As Ever,
(Father's Name)
Mrs. B. B. Ekstrum
Kansas City, Missouri

Christmas Ganders

Enclosed please find a letter from my great-grandfather written to my great-grandmother. He was a Yankee soldier in the Civil War from 1862 to 1865.

Pulaski, Tenn.
December 17, 1863

Sarah E. Brewer
Dear Companion,

Again I am proud of the privilege to write to a bosom friend. This morning is a cold one: the ground is froze very hard, but the master planet (the Sun) is rising as usual in the Eastern horizon, so perhaps by noon the present cold will be more submissive. Yesterday was a very raw day.

Well, Sarah, I sent $45 to be Expressed to you by our Q. M. (Hay). He left here with the money yesterday morning, for Nashville, that being the nearest express office. You will find the money at C. Brown's. There will be some expressage to pay, I don't know how much. If you send any person except your Pa after it, you had better send a written order, lest they would be bothered in getting it.

A couple of days ago when I was on picket, George Strattan, myself, and a couple of men of the 7th Iowa were upon one post. Along about twelve o'clock, the sun shining very warm, George and I concluded to take our guns and walk down to the creek, which was close by. Accordingly we started, upon drawing nigh to the creek, what should we see, but two men sitting on the bank sunning themselves. We quickly halted, gazed at them and saw they were young, genteel-looking fellows. We pronounced them Rebels and immediately concluded to capture them. So George passed slyly to the right and I to the left, and at the same time closing in on them.

We were successful in our undertaking and captured them and took them up to our post and kept them under guard until the next morning. At about relief time, when we took them out of the little

150

obscure place where we put them, we cut their heads off and wrapped them up nicely in our blankets.

What? Did I say men? A mistake, they were ganders, and made a fine roast, too, for our dinners.

Christmas is drawing nigh. I feel quite different now to what I did last December. Perhaps enough, write soon.

Yours, as ever,
E. H. Brewer
Serena Cundall
Glendo, Wyoming

Story Of War From Lost Son

Port Huston, S. C.
January 21, A.D., 1864

My dear friend,

It is with great pleasure that I am permitted this morning to rite you a few lines to let you know that i have not forgotten you, yet tho I am many miles from you while you are at home enjoying the pleasures of life and I am in what is called the sunny south standing the stormes. We will stand the stormes, it won't be long till this cruel war is over.

I am well at this time and the rest of the boys are hoping these few lines may find you in the same state of health. Well, John, I have saw some hard times since I saw you. We have bin in 18 fights, our company has only lost two men in battle. We have bin lucky.

The boys that you know is all well. We have lost a good meney men by sickness. We are at Port Huston. We have bin to New Orleans and 300 miles west of there. When you write, direct your letters to Co. H, 118th Ill.'s Cavalry, Department of the Gulf.

From friend Jesse F. Bennett
To John Savidge

Decatur, Alabama
Apr. 4

Mrs. Savidge,

Sis, I take my pen in hand to Inform you of our Wellfare, and to answer your letter I received a few Days ago. We are all right on the loose. I hope this may find you all the same. Well, the first is, I think, the girls, they had better all marry While they are at it, but there is a few more left yet. Well, what Does the copperhead's folks do for a living since we left? Well, Sis, I would rather have my name recorded and afloat off every treetop In these United States that I was an Abolitionist than to have it said I was opposed to the Administration. After this was done, the copperheads, if they was Down below our line for just one month, would come back the best Union men in the World. I am In hopes they will see their folly after While. Well, enough for this time. It is very Disagreeable today, so no more.

From W. W. Williams, as ever
To George Savidge
Write soon.

Decatur, Alabama
April 4

Dear Father

I thought I would write to you this morning to let you know that I am well, hoping this will find the family the same. It is very muddy here now, it rained all night. It rains about half of the time here now.

We got here the 2nd of March about dark and camped in the woods that night. It snowed all night and in the morning there was about 10 inches of snow. About daylight we got up and marched five miles through the snow and mud. We then went into an old stable and stayed there two days. We have now got barricks built and I expect that we will stay here for some time.

It is a nice place here on the Tennessee river. There is a Rebel force about 20 miles from here of about 8,000, and they are a-coming into our lines at the rate of 30 per day and a great many are enlisting in our Army. This the copperheads can't deny, for I see it myself. I got a letter from Mary the other day. Tell Warren to be a good boy and feed the calves. Want you to all write as often as you can, so I will close for this time.

Decatur
April 26

Dear Father,

I received your letter last night and was glad to hear from you. You said you have been making rails. I should think you was able to hire them made. You said you had sold Ben to Peg. I hope she will take care of him and not trade him off. I do not haft to expose myself very much. The other night I was on picket and it rained allmost all night, but I had my rubber and I did not get much wet. The Rebels still keeps a scare here but I don't think they have any notion of attacking us here. Our scouts are fighting them every day.

The boys are all well. Marlow has not got to the regiment yet, but we are looking for him soon. Is Langley going west this summer and what is he doing this summer? I want you to tell me what regiment Jim Williams in in, there are several Ohio regiments here. I have no news to write, we eat bread and meat here until we want a change and then we eat meat and bread. I will close for this time, write soon.

Decatur
April 29

Dear Brother,

I take this opportunity of writing to you to let you know we are all well and hope this will find you all well. We have marching orders, I guess we will leave the first, which will be the day after tomorrow. I do not know where we will go. There is a man in here in the 43rd Ohio by the name of Budd. I am going to hunt him up tomorrow, he may be some of our relations.

I want you to find out what regiment our folks are in and let me know. Maybe I can find some. I guess I will close for now — have no news to write. You must write and tell me all the news.

Chicamauga Creek, Georgia
May 6, 1864

Dear Brother

As I had a little spare time today I thought I would write to you. I received your letter the 30th and we started the next morning, so this is the first time I have had time to write.

We have traveled 160 miles. We walked about 80 miles. We traveled through the Cumberland Mountains. We camped last night on the Chicamauga battlefield. It was quite a sight for me. The trees were shot off by the hundreds. We passed Lookout Mountain, Mission Ridge and Chattanooga. This country shows war. I don't think we will travel very far for awhile unless the Rebels retreat, for they are only fifteen miles from here. We have a heavy force here. I stood the tramp first rate.

We have plenty to eat, hardtack and sow belly. I can eat a pound of sow belly at a meal. It is a good place here to break boys in. There is not news here so I will close. I want you to write often, for I don't know when I will write again. Direct via Nashville and they will get it here all right.

Saturday, June 30

Sister Lisa,

I for the first time will try to write a few lines to you to let you know how I get along. I am at the hospital, yet, but I am getting along first rate. I am very weak yet. I think I will be able to go to the regiments in about a week. Tom Calihan is here with me, he does not gain very fast. Wilson is here now.

We have moved 15 miles from Heworth. We left the boys there, but I don't expect they are there now. They expected to leave there for the front. There is about 300 sick and wounded here.

We don't live very well here. Liza, if I had a piece of our light bread I could eat it very well. We eat hardtack here. We got soda crackers for dinner, they tasted good to me. Better than any biscuits I ever ate. We get a few dried apples once in awhile. I was out today and gathered some huckleberries and served them. They taste like curns, there is lots of them here.

I guess I will close for this time. I want you all to write often for I like to hear from you — direct to John W. Savidge, 644 Division by via Chattanooga.

> Hospital of the 4th Division
> 15th A. C.
> Allatoona, Georgia, July

Mr. Savidge,

Not being able to write myself I have this morning got a comrade to write a few lines for me. I have been very low for about a month and haven't been writing much myself, but Tommy Calihan has written home regular and has told his folks how John was.

I supposed you would learn from them that John came here with Diareah, and he improved for sometime and got able to get around. He went once to pick some berries and overdone himself and was taken down with fever and has been very low ever since for over a week.

I will not give you any false hopes for I know you would rather know the worst. It is thought that he cannot get well. But still there is Hope as long as there is life. We will write again in a few days and let you know how he is.

It is a long road and very uncertain whether you will get the letters or not, but we will write as often as possible. I believe this is all for this time. You must hope for the best. It is not worthwhile for you to write to us as we are about forty miles from Regiment and would not get your letters.

> Believe me as ever,
> Respectfully Yours,
> Wilson L. Gosnell

Camp near Savannah, Georgia
Dec. 26th, 1864

Kind Friend Mrs. Savidge,

I have just been talking with Thomas Calihan concerning Johnny's affairs as you requested of me and I will write it to you as he told me all he knew concerning Johnny while he was sick.

Concerning his clothing, he had none, only the clothing he had on and was buried in them. He had a blanket, it was turned over to the hospital sturat and Tommy doesn't know what become of it. Tommy says he took care of him most of the time he was sick. He says he doesn't know what became of his pocketbook. Tommy says he had his senses all the time except the last three or four days, when he would call for his mother frequently.

The chaplain of our regiment was with him a good bit while he was sick and was with him when he died and helped to bury him. His name was Wycoff. He is a very fine man and a good minister. He is one of the kindest men I nearly ever knew and is very good and kind to the sick and wounded.

You wished to know of me if safe to go after John. I will say it is in enemies' country and we have no army anywhere near there and there is not railroad within fifty or sixty miles of there. I mean Rome, Georgia, where he is buried. There was a railroad running to Rome, but when the army left that country the railroads were all destroyed, So it would be almost impossible for you to go there and get his body.

In your letter you said Hubert said John was never well after he left Ottawa. That was not true. For awhile he was at Decatur, Alabamy, and he had as good health as ever and for sometime after he left there. I believe I have told you all concerning Johnny, Mrs. Savidge.

156

I am very thankful to you for your kindness in sending socks, although I never received them, but am thankful to you for your kindness. This leaves me in good health, and hoping this may reach you and find you and your family well, so no more, but remaining your friend as ever,

Francis M. Frank
To Mrs. Remembrance Savidge
Submitted by Carmilee Larson
Tennessee, Illinois

Massacre Of Fort Pillow

This is a Civil War letter from my grandfather to his sister.

Camp at Ringgold, Georgia
May the 3rd, 1864

Dear Sister:

I received your letter of April the 23rd and was glad to hear from you all. You may tell Mother she need not be scared about me being vaccinated. I will try and have some Photographs taken as soon as I can. You see there is no place around here where I can have them taken. Them last pens are pretty good ones. They are 9/10 better than the other ones.

We just came off a 10 mile march yesterday, but I was so weak that they had to haul me part of the way so I did not have a very hard time of it. I had been sick with the bloody flux.

We expect to get paid off in a few days. We are encamped in a healthier place than we was before, on a hill where we can see the mountains. They are all covered with green trees. They look very pretty. There is any amount of wildflowers around here, more wild honey sweets than anything else.

We are expecting to have a big fight before long. The Reb pickets are only 3 or 4 miles from here. I suppose you heard about the massacre of Fort Pillow where the Rebs murdered all the prisoners. We have not forgot that yet. When we get to fight we will not take any prisoners either. I expect there won't be any prisoners taken. They will shoot them like dogs, like they did with our men, which will make both sides fight the harder, for they won't surrender for they know they will be shot...

Thomas (older brother) is well and sends his best respects to all the folks. I know of nothing more to write at present. Give my best respects to all the folks except (sic) the same yourself.

George H. Harvey
Robert Harvey
Bartlesville, Oklahoma

Sherman's March Through The Eyes Of A Soldier

My mother was Ella Fagen Robinson (1887-1973). In her possession, she had a series of letters written by her grandfather, Abraham Bennett, during his service with the Second Iowa Infantry, Fourth Division, 15th Army Corp of the Union Army.

October 1864: "John W. Moore and I bunk together. We have a good bed of straw, plenty to eat, plenty of river water to drink. I was put on top of the stagecoach at 8 p.m., where I stayed until daylight. We have two days rations. I haven't been examined; we passed between two doctors and held up our hands; that was all.

"I must tell you what I got — an overcoat; beau pants; two shirts; two drawers; two pair of socks; one fine hat with the eagle-bugle and a fine feather on it; a splendid blanket; and a good oil cloth to keep warm and dry."

"I am at Nashville now in the biggest house I ever saw — five stories from the ground. I am sitting on my knapsack, writing on my knee."

Later: "The big house I was in...in Nashville fell down (two nights after we stayed there). It killed 300 men. You see, I was lucky."

January 8, 1865 — from Savannah, Georgia: "I have got some good hope of going home in the spring. We got the news today that Georgia has called her state militia home."

January 31, 1865 — from the field in Georgia: "We are the dirtiest looking brutes you ever saw after a few days' march...and lousy is no name for the lice. They pretty nearly eat some of us up some nights."

February 10, 1865 — from South Carolina: "We marched 22 miles today...we are sweeping the country of everything — horses, cattle, hogs, flour, meal, potatoes — burning the dwellings; burning up fencing; just cleaning it out."

March 13, 1865 — from North Carolina: "One-third of us is bare-footed; our shoes are worn out, and we can't draw any until we get communications. My boots are worn out so I have to tie them on my feet with pieces of rope."

Abraham Bennett marched in the review of Union troops in Washington, D. C., on May 25, 1865. He received his discharge in July, 1865.

Although Abraham had complained only of blistered feet, and a slight cold during the course of his letters, he had contacted a fatal fever — possibly typhoid or malaria — while in the South, and died at home on Sept. 11, 1866. He was 29 years old.

Hope Robinson
Yale, Iowa

Letter From Vicksburg

My great-grandfather Asahel Mann was in the 15th Army Corps, Co. A, 4th Iowa Cavalry, as was his brother John. In a letter written to his father in Iowa, June 20, 1863, John says, "This morning I seat myself under the shade of a beech tree to write you a few lines. We are all well and in good health. We are on picket about one mile from camp. We are camped 14 miles in the rear of Vicksburg.

"There has been the heaviest firing going on this morning that I have heard since the fight commenced. There is a constant roaring of the cannons.

"Day before yesterday, our company was ordered to charge. We raised the whoop and here we went. They turned the other way and broke for the brush. We had to run through a corn field over very rough ground and over ditches. In running one mile 12 horses fell. My horse fell twice with me. Out of that number of horses falling, there wasn't a man hurt.

We have just got our new arms, Sharpe carbines. We are armed now just as well as any regiment of cavalry, and I think can do just as good fighting."

John Mann

Two days later, in battle near Vicksburg, John Mann was killed. He was 27 years, six months old.

Carol Conner
Colorado Springs, Colorado

S

T

U

W

Z

INDEX